I0570145

THE GOLD STANDARD

Winning Ways with the Mondays

SABRINA AND KENNY MONDAY

Copyright © 2024 Sabrina and Kenny Monday.

ISBN: 979-8-9875656-4-3

All rights reserved. No part of this book may be reproduced, stored, or transmitted by any means—whether auditory, graphic, mechanical, or electronic—without written permission of both publisher and author, except in the case of brief excerpts used in critical articles and reviews. Unauthorized reproduction of any part of this work is illegal and is punishable by law.

Scripture references were taken from the
New Living Testament version of the Bible.

CONTENTS

DEDICATION

For our parents, Alquita and Edward Goodwin Jr.
and Elizabeth and Fred Monday who introduced us
to our faith, the foundation of our belief system.

NOTE TO THE READER

Success can be measured in many ways. Sometimes you might not place, and other times you might get bronze or silver. It's not always about winning the race, but in lessons learned in running the race. Through faith, hard work, and determination, we've been able to thrive and build a golden family legacy. At this stage in life, we've realized part of our purpose is to encourage and motivate others in their lives.

You will sometimes read our individual thoughts and at other times, you will see where we both write as one. If you do not see our names individually attributed to a section or paragraph, that is a representation of our unity on that particular subject.

We both had much to share, as we wanted you to get the panoramic view of our lives together. On the following pages, we hope you can take some of our same principles and apply them to your life so you, too, can be resilient in achieving family success.

Sabrina & Kenny

A MESSAGE FROM GLORIA MAYFIELD BANKS

International Speaker, Entrepreneur and Success Strategist

Kenny and Sabrina individually are strong. Their influence and impact have been deep and wide. I have loved the breadth of those they have impacted. If they move into your neighborhood - *impact*. If they are a part of your professional organization - *impact*. If you are a parent or involved in a child/young adult's life, they take responsibility - *impact*. Women building entrepreneurial ventures, *athletes* in wrestling and all areas of sports - *impact*. BUT TOGETHER - what a force. The lives they have personally touched around the globe as champions themselves and their children, in sports, education, community and personal development gives them a platform that is unique and robust. Their energy, wisdom, and insight blended with experiences that span so many areas are impressive. For so many years, I have watched them grow together as a family, friends, and professional advisors to many world-shakers.

The Mondays, with their immediate and extended family, have made waves as they taught so many others to do the same.

INTRODUCTION
Welcome to Our Journey

Sabrina: I met my husband, Kenny, (back then, known as Kenny Boo), at Booker T. Washington High School, in Tulsa, Oklahoma in 1977. He was an accomplished wrestler and would go on to win Olympic Gold and become a world-class coach. He began wrestling at the age of six, when he followed his two older brothers into the sport, starting in a YMCA afterschool program. The Y was located near Pine and Peoria in Tulsa and is now located on the street bearing his name: "Kenny Monday Place."

Kenny grew up wrestling in Oklahoma, where he won 4 state titles and the 1977 Junior National Championships. His record from 7th to 12th grade was an astonishing 140-0-1. In college, he was a 3x all American wrestler and NCAA Champion in 1984 at Oklahoma State, where his record was 121-12-2.

After college, Kenny won a Gold medal in the 1988 Seoul, Korea Olympics, becoming the first Black man to win a Gold medal in the USA. He also won a Silver medal in Barcelona, Spain, in 1992 and finished 6th in the 1996 Olympic Games in Atlanta, Georgia as the team captain. He won multiple Gold and Silver medals in World Cups, World Championships, and Pan-American events. After retiring from competition, Kenny became a highly respected coach, now Head Wresting Coach at Morgan State University in Baltimore, Maryland, and is a member of the National High School Hall of Fame, National Wrestling Hall of Fame, and the International Wrestling Hall of Fame. Kenny's proud and encouraging parents were witness to his amazing successes.

Married to this awesome man, we have created a happy, love-filled family together, overcoming many obstacles, raising 3 awesome young adults -- 1 daughter and 2 sons, all college-educated: Sydnee, Howard University grad; Kennedy, UNC Chapel Hill grad; and Quincy, Princeton University grad. It hasn't always been easy, but it has always been worth it. I thank God that He connected me to the man of my dreams, perfect for me.

Kenny: Sabrina and I married September 4, 1994. Although we met in high school, we were not high school sweethearts. We knew each other but never dated. (We did flirt a lot though!) Thirteen years after high school graduation, our paths crossed again. I was living in Oklahoma and Sabrina was living in Boston. We started dating long distance, and we were engaged within 6 months and married within the year. The romance was hot, heavy, and moved swiftly. Sabrina says her mom always said, "When you know, you will know." Well, we knew!

Sabrina is a descendant of survivors of the 1921 Tulsa race massacre. She comes from a family of dreamers and doers and is a successful wife, mom, sister, friend, global mentor, and entrepreneur. I am eternally grateful for my beautiful wife's love and unwavering support throughout the years. She has made me a better man. This is no ordinary love.

Sabrina has thrived 30-plus years in direct sales. She has climbed to the top of Mary Kay Cosmetics, Inc., as an Independent National Sales Director, earning the use of 16 pink Cadillacs throughout her career. There are over 1 million independent beauty consultants worldwide in Mary Kay Cosmetics, Inc. and only approximately 150 active National Sales Directors in the United States. Sabrina previously hosted a daily radio show, where she continued to bring out the best in people, helping them to tap into their God-given gifts through belief and education while encouraging them to grow mentally, spiritually, and financially.

She always says, "When you are a better woman to yourself, you are better for everybody else." Judging by her career, our family, and our life together, she's right!

Sabrina and Kenny: Throughout this book, we'll *pass the microphone* (on the page) back and forth, like we just did above. We will be sharing real-life experiences and lessons we've learned along the way to creating power and success individually and collectively as a family. We don't have it all together, but together, we have it all.

This is a true American success story that fuels the soul. We've learned to be focused, bold, and intentional. We are goal-getters and full of faith. We have been blessed to travel the world to over 40 foreign countries, believing to change the world, you must see the world. We have worked to believe in ourselves and believe in each other. The fundamentals we'll share in this book have been our blueprint for success, and we hope they help you build your own. When options and opportunities present themselves, you must make the moments matter.

FAITH

Kenny: One of the earliest memories of my faith being tested and the importance of believing and relying on my faith to overcome a very difficult time in my life was when I was about 10 years old. I had been wrestling for 4 years and was really starting to fall in love with the sport. It was 1972, and the Summer Olympic Games was 7 months away. This was the first time I really understood that winning an Olympic Gold medal was the ultimate prize in the sport. There was no professional league that a wrestler could go into after their amateur career, so it was the Olympics or nothing.

It was a very exciting time to be a wrestler. The 1972 Olympic Team was getting a lot of coverage on TV, primarily because of the legendary Dan Gable, who went on to win Olympic Gold that summer. I was more inspired and felt really connected because I had the opportunity to watch the members of the Olympic Team compete at the USA National Wrestling Tournament in Stillwater, OK, on the campus of Oklahoma State University (OSU).

I had begun to make a name for myself in Oklahoma, one of the hot beds of wrestling. I had started wrestling at the YMCA on the north side of Tulsa; we were one of the few all-Black wrestling teams in the city in a predominantly white sport. Tulsa in the '70s was still a highly segregated city, and our team was faced with some resistance when we showed up to compete in the tournaments. There were times that our team manager would register the team, but when we arrived ready to compete, the tournament director would say there was some mistake. The team hadn't been registered, and so we were not allowed to compete. This happened more than a few times. Our coach and parents would insistently fight for the team to wrestle. After unfair resistance they would eventually allow us to compete.

In my 30-year career in the sport of wrestling, there have only been a few times that I considered quitting the sport. Along with the tournament directors trying to keep us from competing, some of the referees would make horrible calls against our team, causing us to lose matches that we should have won. When I was around ten years old, the time that really made me want to give the sport up was in the City Championship. I had worked my butt off to prepare for one of the biggest tournaments of the year. I had come close the previous year to winning before losing in the semifinals to the defending state champ. This year was going to be different.

I had worked all summer in order to be at my best for this tournament. Me and the same kid, the defending state champ, met this year in the finals. We were both undefeated, having great seasons. The match started, and I was off to a good start, outwrestling the kid in every position. The referee made bad call after bad call, clearly biased in the other kid's favor. It was evident that some of the fans—who weren't even pulling for me—started to boo the referee.

When the final whistle blew and the match was over, the other wrestler was declared the winner 10–8. I was so disappointed—not by the way I performed but by the way the ref called the match. Although I was somewhat used to referees making biased calls against me and our team, the clear prejudice made it extremely difficult to win. This one was the tipping point for me.

Many kids and parents, both White and Black, came

up to me and apologized for the ref, saying I had won that match. After the tournament, I was in tears, and I told my parents that I wanted to quit the sport and go play basketball with some of my other friends. It was obvious that some of the parents and kids didn't want us there, and the referees were making it so hard to win that it just wasn't fair. I was done and didn't see any reason to continue going to practice to work hard just to come to the tournaments and get treated that way.

As a 10-year-old kid, I didn't know much about racism and couldn't understand why it was happening. One of my parents' house rules, with not many exceptions, was that if we started something, we would have to finish the season. For me, this was one of those exceptions. Those situations and the people behind them were taking the fun out of the sport and killing the passion that I was starting to develop. This was a critical moment in my life.

My parents sat me down and reiterated the importance of my faith. They reminded me that God made everyone in His image. No man or woman is better than you solely because of the color of their skin.

"There will probably always be racist people that will try to keep you from doing what you love," they said. "You can't let them defeat you and keep you from becoming who you want to be."

My mother encouraged me to keep my head up and never let anyone steal my joy. My dad told me to pray and ask God to give me the strength to overcome and to lead me in the direction He wanted me to go. My parents and coaches assured me they would handle the refs and tournament directors; that was their fight, not mine. I just had to keep working hard, keep believing in myself and if, at the end of the season, I still wanted to quit the sport, they would have no problem.

My faith and the support from my parents and coaches were enough for me to try again, and I won the next championship and the one after that. Through years of working hard, believing in myself and my support system, I went on to become a 3x Olympian, bringing home a Gold medal in 1988 from Seoul, Korea and a Silver medal in 1992 from Barcelona, Spain.

Faith is all about letting go of control, doing the right thing, and knowing that it will eventually work out. You still have to work hard, but that work feels less difficult with the support that faith gives you. Faith is important because it helps you know right from wrong. Our faith in Jesus Christ, who is our Lord and Savior, has given us a system to live by. It gives us foundational principles to help us make better decisions. But most of all, it gives us discipline to face hardships and not give up.

DISCIPLINE

Discipline has been the cornerstone of our foundation. Discipline teaches obedience, as does faith. When you teach your children Godly submission, you are teaching them to do the right thing for all the right reasons. And teaching yourself discipline helps you make the right decisions later in life with your family and in business. Although faith supports your own sense of discipline, you have to build that discipline for yourself. You must move beyond simply obeying and reach a point where you want to make good decisions for yourself, your family, your business, and your community on a foundation of love and trust. This is internal discipline as opposed to external discipline.

Discipline supports your ability to stay the course in whatever you do. True discipline, supported by faith, requires a strong work ethic, self-motivation, and vision. It also allows you to build those crucial aspects of success and is rewarded by good results. The more disciplined you are, the more you'll want to live a disciplined life and the easier it will become. Discipline affords organization and order, which sets you free to be creative and productive.

Patience is a form of discipline. It's easy to know that achieving a large goal will take time, but it is much harder to actually embrace that concept. We all have to overcome impatience and accept that good things will come in time, if you are willing to put in the required work.

Another foundational strength is your mindset.

You must be intentional in creating a winning mindset. Having a mindset of positivity drives you forward. We call this the *Champion Mindset.*

To train your brain into this new mindset, you will need focus, daily work, and time. You must focus on the mundane tasks and do them over and over. Creating great habits don't come overnight. Force yourself to work on the one thing that will make you great every single day; that's what it takes to be a champion.

No one gets to the Olympics by practicing only on the weekends.

In the end, your thoughts control your actions. Discipline in all areas creates success that gives you satisfaction. At times in our lives, we have failed to align with the standards we have set for ourselves, and those are the times when our daily disciplines, such as prayer or meditation, have been out of order. Even when you are disciplined and life's outcomes don't seem to be going your way, a champion mindset gives you a perspective of positivity, of winning. That puts you in a powerful position to continue to push past the disappointments.

TOOLS OF DISCIPLINE

Here are a few spiritual tools of discipline that have helped us over the years.

Prayer and Quiet Time

Sabrina and Kenny: We work to carve out this time daily. We read from our daily devotionals and work from our prayer journals. These daily devotions at the top of our morning center us. That time together gives us the armor of God, giving us peace and protection. This disciplined approach to mindfulness and devotion to each other and to God has helped shape and manage our lives.

Sabrina: We have a ritual we have used for years: I open with prayer, and Kenny reads from the scripture of the day. Then we study and discuss that Bible passage to gain a better understanding. We look for ways the passage can be applied to our everyday living. I then read a passage from one of our devotionals. We discuss it and go to the scripture that supports the Bible reading. Sometimes we play our favorite gospel music; that always sets the tone. Kenny always closes us out with prayer.

This daily discipline has strengthened our marriage and has gotten us through tough times. Without it, our marriage, and even our family, possibly could not have survived. The discipline to take the necessary time for important study together has made the difference. When our lives get busy and we don't connect through our study time together, we both feel disconnected from each other and from ourselves. Our discipline for prayer and devotion has been paramount to our family's success.

Sabrina and Kenny: We have become a praying family. There have been times throughout our marriage where our prayer life was stronger than others, but we've

committed to growing that part of our life and supporting each other through it.

We have learned to lean on God's unchanging hands
to navigate life. Sometimes life gets so big, we have just
had to trust God. When you have done all you can, we
have learned to put that problem, that issue, in God's box.
Let Him handle it. That allows us to not be consumed by
something that is out of our control. We love that God's
email doesn't get full. His voicemail is never full, and His
line is never busy. He is always available and an instant
source of comfort and understanding. God says, "Give all
your worries and cares to God, for he cares about you,"
(1 Peter 5:7), and so we do.

God wants a relationship with us, but not out of con-
venience. He wants us to be close. We have to make ourselves available at all times to Him through prayer and
relationship, (not just in emergency situations), just as
He is available to us. It takes discipline to make the time
for God, but if He can make the time for us, we can do
it for Him.

God is a forgiving God. We loved our motto at our
church in South Florida, the church by the Glades, pastored by David Hughes: "No perfect people allowed." We

have fallen off our schedule many times, but we always find ourselves getting back on track because it has been beneficial throughout our marriage. You don't have to be perfect; just start somewhere. For some, it's five minutes a day; for others, it's hours of your day. For us, we pray throughout the day -- in the car, at a wrestling tournament, before a business meeting -- not just before a meal or at night.

Sabrina: I was taught as little girl to say a nightly prayer, and I still do it: "Now I lay me down to sleep. I pray the Lord my soul to keep. If I should die before I wake, I pray the Lord my soul to take. God bless Mama, Daddy, sister, brothers." Even though my parents are deceased, I still recite that prayer, and it settles my soul. It gives me a closeness to my Lord and Savior and gives me a sense of peace and protection.

Kenny: One of our key examples of the power of our faith happened in our first year of marriage, in 1994, when we were planning on buying our first home together. I had just completed the sale of my house in Stillwater, OK, and felt good with how fast it sold. I felt even better because I sold the home for $20k more than I purchased it in only three years of ownership, so we had a good down payment, including the sale of a couple of toys I had acquired (a motorcycle and a Corvette). Sabrina and I believed we could go to the bank and not have an issue getting a mortgage for the beautiful home we had decided on, after looking at a ton.

The home buying process can be exhausting and challenging, first, trying to decide on where you want to reside and what part of the city you want to live and factoring in the school district you want to someday educate your kids in. It took us several months searching over 60 homes before finally choosing a home that we really liked. We thought it was the perfect first home to raise a family. It was in a great neighborhood, and the housing development was only a few years old. The school district was one of the best in the city, and the house was only a short, five-minute drive from the elementary school.

To our surprise, the first couple of banks we spoke with to try and secure the loan for the house turned us down. The first bank said we should try a much smaller home that would be a little less expensive. The second bank said we didn't have enough established credit together. One of the bank's loan officers suggested we try leasing a home until we could raise our credit scores.

Feeling confused and a little dejected, I remember sitting in the kitchen of Sabrina's mother's house and thinking about *what do we do next?* Sabrina and I talked about it and decided to not give up on the house we had picked, to keep believing that we could find a bank that would work with us and give us the loan. We prayed and relied on our faith in God to see us through.

Once we handed the responsibility over to God, the very next bank we spoke to gave us the loan and at a better rate than the other banks had offered. We were so excited that we were going to purchase our first home together, and it was a clear testament of our faith of not letting a few setbacks kill our dream or lead us to a decision that we would have regretted later.

If you don't have a strong prayer life and don't know where to start, seek a great church home and find small group bible studies to help strengthen your prayer life. It also helps to have a praying wife, a praying mom, and/or others -- someone to remind you to pray or to help you remember why prayer is important. Work to establish your faith community by connecting through your church, family members, and friends.

Spending time to attend church, to read the Bible, to study, worship, and praise creates a strong faith-filled life. You connect with other people and are inspired through their testimonies of how God allowed them to overcome great obstacles in their lives.

We learned not to just pray when it's convenient or when we are asking for God's attention. Pray with praise and thanksgiving daily. We tend to go to God, on bended knee, when there is trouble. But God wants to be the center of our lives all the time.

My childhood pastor, Rev. Leroy K. Jordan, at First Baptist Church North Tulsa, and the father of my best childhood friend, Valerie, would end every Sunday service by saying, "Trust God. Be yourself. Live one day at a time." I have used that as a guiding light in my life.

Fasting

Sabrina and Kenny: Fasting is a cleansing, physically and mentally. It gives you clarity and focus. Sometimes, we'll avoid eating until the afternoon, fasting through the early hours of the day. Sometimes that morning fast will last for 30 days. In a wrestling family, the athletes have to make weight for competition. So fasting to work toward a desired goal was a norm in our household.

Fasting improves alertness, mood, discipline, and overall feelings of well-being.

Your five senses become keener, sharper, while fasting. It gives you a clear direction and lessens indecisiveness. Making a sacrifice by denying yourself food also gives you the ability to receive God's blessings through spiritual nourishment instead.

Gratitude

In this stage and age of life, we have come to a place to appreciate the simple things in life. We now appreciate that less is more. We don't need the excess material things we once thought most important. We now place a high value on health and well-being. Let's be clear: We still love nice things; however, we have a deep appreciation for a walk in the park or a long Sunday drive. We embrace simple activities that quiets the chaos and reduces confusion in our lives. We don't need lots of people in our path, just a few good people we enjoy surrounding ourselves with. We focus on peace and contentment and find simple ways to experience those feelings every day.

Journaling

Habakkuk 2:2 says, "Write my answer plainly on tablets, so that a runner can carry the correct message to others." The instruction is clear: WRITE IT DOWN.

When you see your vision, your plans, your thoughts, your goals, your dreams laid out in front of you on paper or even on a screen, they are easier to execute. When you journal, your thoughts become clearer.

Sabrina: I started this book by journaling and many of the other big goals I've managed to hit, each started with a journal entry. Do not despise small beginnings. By writing down your goals, you can begin to see ways to reach them. You can also write down your blessings, which remind you why you have goals in the first place. I write about my health, my mind, and the peaks and valleys of life.

I like pretty journals, colorful journals, journals that inspire me to write with a positive thought on the front, but some are just a basic spiral notebook. Find a journal that you feel comfortable with and inspired by and then fill it up with your thoughts.

Journaling frees up your mind to focus on other things. You must have a brain dump. That's what I consider my journal. I must still my thought process somehow and writing things down releases them from my brain so I can better focus on the task or thought with clarity. Sometimes, when I'm busy, my assistant helps by jotting down my thoughts for me as I speak them aloud. Journaling allows you to empty your brain, to declutter your thought process. Journaling organizes my thoughts and my prayer life.

Our faith is bulletproof. Nothing can happen in this life that will separate me from God. "And I am convinced that nothing can ever separate us from God's love. Neither death nor life, neither angels nor demons, neither our fears for today nor our worries about tomorrow—not even the powers of hell can separate us from God's love. No power in the sky above or in the earth below—indeed, nothing in all creation will ever be able to separate us from the love of God that is revealed in Christ Jesus our Lord" (Romans 8:38–39). This means that you should simply know that God is God, no matter what you are going through.

Kenny: My faith and belief in God have always been a part of my life growing up. My parents and grandparents were instrumental in introducing me to religion, taking me to church and Bible study on Sunday mornings. But it wasn't until I reached high school that I really started to understand the importance of developing a personal relationship with God. I couldn't depend on or expect anyone else to get that for me.

I had just turned 16 and was starting to drive, so with that privilege came a different level of responsibility. After winning State titles my freshman and sophomore years, going undefeated in both seasons, I was starting to get recruited by every major college wrestling program in the country. The advice I received from just about every coach was to make good decisions, do well in the classroom, stay out of trouble, and keep winning! The hardest part of my success was to separate myself from things, people, and places that would negatively affect my career.

It was during this period of my life that I started to learn more about my faith and to study more intently the principles of Christianity. The more I prayed and fought to stay disciplined in my commitment to my beliefs, the stronger I became in all areas of my life.

Fast forward to my senior year in high school. I had to rely on my faith as it was severely tested. My parents' marriage was falling apart, and they were headed for a separation. It was a very uncomfortable time in the house and trying to navigate through their issues became increasingly more difficult. I was being pulled in both directions, each parent trying to get me to understand their point of view.

I really had no one else to talk to that could help me get through, so I relied on my faith in God and stayed prayerful and focused on school and wrestling. I couldn't control what was going to happen with my parents, but I could control my success and my dream of wrestling in college.

Sabrina: Early on in my childhood, I was grateful for praying grandparents who made us go to church. I remember being sent to my mom's parents' house in Cherryvale, Kansas, every summer, the day after school was out. Without fail, every Sunday, we were in those church pews, sucking on a peppermint. We went to Bible study, songfest, and whatever else was happening at the church house. Yes, I was exposed to the Lord's teaching early on.

My grandparents on my dad's side were also spiritual, especially my grandmother. When we visited them (most of time with sister, brothers, and cousins there too), we attended a little white clapboard Baptist Church in Alsuma, Oklahoma.

We would tell grandmother that we didn't have church clothes, and she quickly quipped, "God doesn't care what you wear to church, as long as you are going." So off to church we went in shorts, a T-shirt, and sandals.

She was determined to get Jesus' word etched deep inside our souls. I am grateful that we were encouraged to embrace God's Word and His love for us at a young age. I learned to believe that nothing is impossible with God by your side. As I grew in my faith, I learned to depend on God's word to pull me up and out of any situation. I was able to love better, to understand scripture, and to apply it in life. Life can be a tangled web; the Word helps detangle it.

After 35 years of marriage, our faith has been tested, but we have always had great faith. The Bible teaches us to have the faith of a mustard seed when we have nothing else. ""You don't have enough faith," Jesus told them. "I tell you the truth, if you had faith even as small as a mustard seed, you could say to this mountain, 'Move from here to there,' and it would move. Nothing would be impossible." (Matthew 17:20).

One of the most challenging times in our marriage was when Kenny went to train in Arizona to make his third Olympic team. I had my multimillion-dollar Mary Kay (MK) business. Plus, we had our Subway franchise and our coffee shop, Monday Morning, both located on UCAT Tulsa college campus and our daughter to raise. It was a tough time, long days, and lots of responsibilities. I made it through only with the grace of God. Faith gave me the strength to get through and overcome those various obstacles.

Faith is the glue holding everything we are, do, and have together. Our strength, our resilience to bounce back, comes from our faith. We don't approach any affair in our lives without guidance from our God, our Alpha and Omega.

Without the Test, There is No Testimony

Sabrina: Faith has allowed me to have a full, busy, productive life. My life's principle has always been that

I can do all things through Christ, who strengthens me. (Philippians 4:13). I remember the times I have felt over-whelmed with so much going on. When our children were small, Kenny was competing and traveling the world. I was busy building my business and there never seemed to be enough hours in the day. When we had a 4- year-old and a 9-month-old, we found out we were expecting another baby and had to navigate it all.

God has put many great people in our lives over the years: our immediate family has always been supportive of our endeavors, along with super support in home and office to keep all the balls in the air. Debbie Pullum has been my smart, charismatic Executive Administrator for 25 plus years. She is my number one confidante and friend.

She helps me know up from down most days. Her cool, calm, collected manner has helped me weather many a storm. Who do you let into your mind, your house, your life? Many people don't trust and, therefore, don't get the support necessary to create a successful life. I learned early on that I cannot be all things to all people. My decision for my immediate family might not be popular with our extended family, but I had to be confident in the decisions I made for us. I remember Kenny's Grandmother asking me at dinner one evening if I planned to slow down now that I was having all these babies. I politely said, "No ma'am," as I looked at Kenny.

Quiet the chatter and calm the chaos in your mind; stop caring about what everybody else thinks works for your life.

My style of discipline is to work with a family calendar, managing many competing priorities successfully, while creating harmony in the household, which was of great importance. Trusting God with our lives, knowing He knows every detail and trusting the process got us through. We've been reminded many times that we are full of capacity, and the average person only uses a small portion of what they are capable of. For me, the only way to handle a big, God-given life is to create a faith-based discipline that gives you order, courage, confidence, and a work ethic to seek excellence in all areas. Clearly, we stumble from time to time in building the family structure. We fall down, but we don't stay down. Life continues to be a juggling act and figuring out things along the way is what we have learned over the years.

Life is a journey, with many ups and downs. There will be losses - - loss of loved ones, loss of jobs, and loss of relationships. When life becomes a lot to bear, for me, that's always been when I've turned to God and my faith. Nothing soothes the soul like the Word and promises of God. When you don't know who to talk to or what to say about a problem you are confronted with in life, for me, my quiet prayer time and a good sermon have given me solace. God is my confidant, with no judgment.

My faith has gotten me through many tough times. I'm grateful. Our life has been blessed tremendously. Without the test, there is no testimony. There have been times in my life when situations would have me fleeing instead of forging ahead. My deep faith allows me to dig deeper, to fight through the pain, to find the purpose. I cling to Deuteronomy 31:6: "So be strong and coura- geous! Do not be afraid and do not panic before them. For the Lord your God will personally go ahead of you. He will neither fail you nor abandon you."

Notes/Reflections

FOCUS

Sabrina and Kenny: We've all been in the zone at one point or another, focused on a task, being highly productive and effective. But focusing is, many times, easier said than done. We had to learn how to eliminate distractions to become successful in life. In today's society, there is a lot of noise, information, and communication coming at you all the time through social media, 24-hour news cycles, and phones that have become a part of our being. You must become good at silencing the noise, quieting your space to think clearly. In order to succeed at any goal you must stay on course and learn to eliminate distractions to become successful.

Sabrina: Blocking out the noise of the world also helps by creating a quiet space. When the world is noisy, you must quiet your mental space to think yourself clear. That requires a peaceful environment, closing the door, separating yourself from others, turning off background noise, the radio, the television, and other people's chatter. Allow yourself to hear from God. You cannot listen if you cannot hear. Turn down the volume on outside noise.

When I need to focus, I am best in a quiet environment. I still marvel at the people who choose to work in Starbucks. That environment is too busy for me - the music, the people, the comings and goings. I find it distractive. Do what works for you.

Perhaps some folks are stimulated by that environment. However you must focus, find it!

Sabrina: My first big test of focusing was attending Tennessee State University (TSU), a Historically Black College and University in Nashville, Tennessee. It was awesome. I felt empowered. There were so many uplifting, intelligent people aspiring to do big things.

But they also loved to party. I'm talking morning, noon, and night. There was always fun to be had, and I had to learn to focus if I wanted a degree in 4 years. Many times, it was the library instead of the party—often the unpopular choice. While others were going left, I had to choose right. When there was a floor party in the dorm, cards were being played, music was blasting, I had to find a quiet corner to do my work.

After TSU, I went on to Boston University to pursue my master's degree in broadcast journalism. It was totally different from my undergrad experience. There, I was the only Black person in my program. I had to invite myself into a study group, because no one was inviting me in. It was lonely at times, and I had to focus on doing more than most to get a decent grade. It was a great time to grow myself up.

The city was cold, the people were cold, and my learning environment was cold, but I focused on becoming better. I took full responsibility. This Oklahoma girl, matriculating on the East Coast, had to find a way to make her own way, and my focus was intense. There was no coddling. Every day, I reaffirmed my intent, and I made a conscious effort to get better daily and to push past my insecurities. I learned to focus on my strengths and not my weaknesses, so that I could keep moving forward.

My Aunt Carmen, who was a television journalist at WHDH in Boston, allowed me to live with her while I attended grad school at Boston University. I had never been on public transportation before, so when I arrived, I asked her about getting to campus.

She quickly gave me a map and a schedule of the T (the local transit system). If I didn't focus on learning the transit system in a new city - - the oldest transit system in America -- I'd still be lost. Navigating my daily transportation took focus. I had to use the map to figure out how to take a bus to the Red Line train and took the Red Line to the Green Line to Kenmore Station. This girl from the Southwest had to focus on not getting swallowed up in the big city and thrive in a new environment.

I focused on becoming independent, working two jobs, and going to school. One of my first jobs was at the *New York Times* call center, selling subscriptions. I never got so many hang-ups in all my life. I had to focus on the customer, basically begging them to buy a subscription. (It was commission based.) I had to focus on my *why*, on my bigger purpose of getting through school. The job was a means to an end, but it was also pretty cool telling people I worked for the *New York Times*...without giving up too many details. Let's examine some areas of focus.

THE POWER OF FOCUS

Kenny: Focus is concentrating on your goals. It's the implementation of the plan you have set to achieve those goals to find success. Focus is important because it allows you to eliminate distractions, to make the best use of your time. What I have realized is that when I'm focused, it helps me to have clear thoughts and to remove clutter and negativity.

It also helps me to say, "No." saying no is a part of focus. To achieve your goals, it is especially important to say no to people who might lead you in the wrong direction, to negative situations, or to things that will move you further from your goals. For example, after I won Olympic Gold, I had many requests and opportunities to teach wrestling clinics and to speak at engagements, which would mean making a great income. The downside was that it required travel and would take me away from my training schedule.

In the beginning, the money was difficult to pass up, and I soon found that my training was compromised, and my performance suffered. I competed in the 1989 US Open not in the best shape. It was my first national tournament after my success at the Olympics, and I should have been at the top of my game. But I struggled through the tournament. I ended up withdrawing from the competition after biting my tongue in the quarterfinals, which required 15 stitches.

I was focused, but it wasn't on wrestling. I was more focused on making money and traveling to more training camps and speaking engagements. It became more of a distraction trying to keep up with my schedule.

I made the decision to refocus on wrestling and that included saying no to business opportunities and people wanting me to come speak. That decision paid off; my focus became better, and my training returned to where it needed to be. I went on to make the world team and won a world title that year.

You can build focus by scheduling your daily tasks. It helps me to have a to-do list every day, even if I have only a few things to get done. One thing my dad would always preach to me was to take care of business before pleasure, so those words constantly ring in my head. I make sure to focus on accomplishing the most important things first, then follow up with things with lower priority. It takes discipline to stay focused on a daily basis, but it helps you to accomplish goals and stay on track.

PAY ATTENTION

The flip side of blocking noise is giving your full attention. Paying attention is like meditation: you have to be in the moment. If you find your mind wandering, you must have the know-how to regain your focus.

Focus on the Focus! (This is a Kenny'ism, which is a phrase coined by Kenny). I'm best when I'm not heavily multitasking. Of course, most successful people can juggle a handful of tasks well. However, be careful not to be overcommitted or overwhelmed. Stay on task.

MAKE THE HARD CHOICE

It can be difficult, but in order to focus, you often have to make the hard or unpopular choice. That might mean saying no to the party or coffee with friends when you have work to do.

Sabrina: When we started a family, my energy level was no longer the same for engaging with other people and outside activities. The children took (and deserved) a lot; therefore, the many volunteer gigs and professional organizations that I was a part of had to fall to the side. Many couldn't understand why I no longer did the things I had been doing, but you have to be ok with outgrowing people, places, and things. Don't allow society to define you; you define your society. I've always lived by this mantra. My life works, people, and things work around it.

FIND SUPPORT

Find your tribe, the people who take you higher. Show me your friends, and I'll show you your future. Most of us are the sum of the five people we hang out with.

Reach up and out—in your church, your work, your business, your teammates. Link with people you respect and admire and who hold you accountable.

If you are the sharpest pencil in the tin, you are not in a growth environment. You should always be a great student, and you can't do that if you aren't challenged or looking for a lesson. There is always something to learn from somebody.

I was blessed to have mentors who guided me along the way, like Dr. Sandra Holt, then a professor in the esteemed honors program at Tennessee State University. She took great interest in my achievements. She cared very much and told me that if I made good choices, I could be great. Dr. Holt was just joy, always smiling, always positive, always bringing a you-can-do-it attitude to the classroom.

When I was invited into the honors program, I was interviewed by Dr. Holt. She explained the benefits of the program and encouraged me into leadership roles on campus. She also shared the work that would be expected of me. If selling the program was her job, she was great at it. She talked about this program as a way of setting me apart from others on campus and how it would look great on my resume. For an incoming freshman, all of the perks were attractive.

She was right. Being part of this program allowed me to set academic standards for myself, which gave me the confidence to be a candidate for Miss Freshman and to go on to be very involved in leadership throughout my college career.

It was Dr. Holt's belief in me that always spurred me on to be better. The words we give to young aspiring minds mean more to them than we think. I'm grateful for her leadership and mentorship. We are good friends to this day, and she is still an empowering and encouraging influence on my life.

Drs. Jamie and Mac Williams were a husband-and-wife team, professors who ran the communications department at TSU. They were very accomplished in academia, and they were also great role models. They showed me what focus and commitment could bring you.

The Williamses were both icons in the Nashville community. They took me under their wings, stretched me, told me to never settle in life. They were role models in every way, such as their 75-year marriage. They were not only amazing professors, but they loved their students as if they were their own children. They were the kind of mentors who would give you the grade you deserved—good or bad—then cook dinner for you.

They had a way of building confidence by being open, honest, and fair and allowing you to do the same, building you up in every way possible. They were always uplifting and loving. Even in their correction, you knew they wanted the best for you. Excellence was their gold standard. You wanted to make them proud.

Dr. McDonald Williams, affectionately known as Dr. Mac, died at the age of 101 ½. He certainly left his mark on the world. He founded the honors program at TSU, was the first director, and he ran the program for 23 years; he was a man of a few words, however, when he spoke, every word was impactful. His calm, resolute ways made you sit a little taller and speak with clarity. He spent 30 years at the university as an English professor. His legacy as an academic genius continues to inspire generations through the TSU honors program.

Dr. Jamye Williams lived to be 102. On her 100th birthday, all she wanted was for people to give 100 dollars to her alma mater, Wilberforce University, through a GoFundMe account. Some of her former students include Oprah Winfrey, Leontyne Price, Wilma Rudolph, Dr. Bobby Jones, Dr. Glenda Baskin Glover, and numerous other African Methodist Episcopal (AME) bishops, and college presidents. She was the first woman to hold a major general officer position in the AME Church.

I'm grateful for the people who have poured into my life and those who I can learn from every day. I'm grateful for those who have called me out to be better. I now mentor thousands of entrepreneurs in my sales organization and I learn just as much from them as they do from me. It is amazing how your words and actions can change the trajectory of someone's life. Find people who do that for you and pay it forward.

DO THE WORK

Kenny: Take it upon yourself to be in control of your career. Wherever you are on your journey, you will have a certain degree of control pertaining to your goals you have set. Everyone can work hard but not everyone can work smart. Part of the journey and, in my opinion, the most important part, is to know yourself. You must be brutally honest with yourself and learn and understand your strengths and weaknesses.

Next, is to get the knowledge! You must, if you can, get the right coach or training environment that will best help you to overcome your weaknesses and make them your strengths! The bottom line is, it's hard to teach what you don't know and very difficult to lead where you haven't been. Once you get a grasp on what you need to get better and improve, you will then be able to focus on your areas of concentration and work from intelligence.

Have a *no-excuse* attitude. Belief will always overcome what you see. It doesn't matter where you start, it matters where you finish, so do not be discouraged if the work is not moving as fast as you would like. Keep showing up and anticipate breakthroughs on a daily basis.

Take it upon yourself to be a self-starter. Don't wait for the next person to get things done. Leaders lead! It's the small things that make the biggest difference. For instance, if I show up and the mats aren't clean, for whatever reason, I'm going to get the mop out and start cleaning them myself. It must be done, so don't wait on someone else. Get it done! Don't allow anything that you can control get in the way of getting in your work.

Finally, be consistent! Smart work only moves you forward with repetition. It's similar to a basketball player shooting and practicing hundreds of free throws before it becomes almost automatic. Your percentages greatly improve when you put that consistency behind the work.

All of these pieces work together to help you arrive at your goals. Nothing will just fall in your lap; you have to know what you want, then make good choices, do the work, and pursue that goal over other things, like partying, hanging out, and seeking immediate gratification.

HOW TO FOCUS

Sabrina: There have been times in life when our focus had to be greater than others. It was imperative that I strongly focused as Kenny decided to come out of re-tirement in the mid-1990s. He was going to attempt to make his third Olympic team. That entailed moving to Phoenix, AZ, to train full time.

We talked about the big picture, about him moving, us staying in Oklahoma, and traveling back and forth. We talked about the businesses, the marriage, the kid, the Olympics. We talked about it all. However, in theory, real life never looks like the plan. So, we decided to embrace the move and adjust the sails for the winds that would blow our way throughout the process. We trusted each other, we trusted the process, and most importantly, we trusted God.

Our personalities are similar; neither of us is an over-thinker. We are feelers. That's not always great, but we have felt our way through many situations over the years. We pretty much jump in—sink or swim. They say oppo-sites attract but not in our case. We are more alike than different, and together, we swim more than we sink.

After much prayer, discussion, and contemplation, off to Arizona Kenny went. I'm happy to report that his work was not in vain. He did qualify for his third Olympic Games in 1996 in Atlanta, Georgia. He didn't earn a medal this time, but I am so proud of his valiant efforts. To come out of retirement and make the team was a huge victory all by itself.

During his absence, we had to focus. He was training hard, and I was juggling many balls in the air. There were many days that I didn't know if I was going or coming. I do know my days had to be focused for me to be productive and successful. They went like this: Early to rise with baby duties, then I'd have to make sure the stores were staffed and running smoothly, that payroll was met, and that I was keeping my Mary Kay sales team performing at a high level.

To keep myself motivated and productive throughout the days, I'd make sure I surrounded myself with great help in every area of my life and counted down the days until we'd go visit Phoenix every 3–4 weeks or Kenny would come home.

To create a success strategy, I made lots of lists, organized tasks, and wrote down who was responsible for doing what. This eliminated wasted time and enabled me to manage my time. I love working in a focused zone. I feel in control. When I'm not focused, I feel out of control, so I use the following tactics to keep myself focused.

SET REASONABLE EXPECTATIONS
FOR YOURSELF

You must set reasonable expectations for yourself. Setting reasonable expectations for yourself is a learned behavior. Look at what must be done, not what you'd like to get done. Be clear about the tasks at hand. Work with a deadline that works for you. Yes, stretch yourself, but don't stretch so far you pull a muscle. "Frustration is often misplaced expectation," as stated so eloquently by another mentor and great friend, Gloria Mayfield Banks, who recruited me into Mary Kay. She went on to become the number one income producer in North America with Mary Kay Cosmetics, Inc.

Work with the end in mind. If you're always working toward a goal, that sense of purpose will drive you to be a finisher.

ASK FOR HELP

Help is necessary. I learned early on as a newlywed and an entrepreneur who didn't have a traditional 9 to 5 that I didn't need to be all things to all people. We made sure the businesses were properly staffed so they could run while I was off doing something else. Kenny had family members step in while he was away, and I made sure that I had great help in the home.

We have always had a nanny when the kids were young, plus great babysitters. I believe in paying for quality child-care. As parents, we had full, busy lives, traveled a great deal, and it was our preference that the children had a stable home environment. I usually found our best help through the referral system, asking people we knew from church and business. I've also gone through an au pair agency. We have always been a fun, crazy, loving family. People were attracted to our lively household and liked being a part of the Monday adventures. We even had one nanny leave her family for a year and move from Oklahoma to Texas with us. God bless Marvalene; not sure what we would have done without her. I'm so grateful for her and other caretakers who helped care for the children and manage the house over years. There was Miss Ratliff, Miss Crump, Miss Joyce and Melisha. They made such a difference.

God blessed us with kind, loving people to help create the life we desired. I am an avid believer that God will give you what you need when you need it. Help is all around, and you must be specific in what you want. When I looked for childcare in the home, I wanted the candidate to be loving, kind, patient, older, a nonsmoker, trustworthy, and to have no young children of her own. Anyone who is hired to work with you and/or your children —at home or in the office—should be confident in their abilities.

DEFINE YOUR EXPECTATIONS OF OTHERS

Enroll the players who are necessary to getting the job done. Be clear in your communication of what is expected of them. Don't assume the players know what to do. Give them precise instructions and an idea of what success looks like to you.

Create focus groups, if necessary, to discuss the plan of action.

CREATE A DISTRACTION-FREE ZONE

I love going into a room, a part of the house, and sitting down to focus on a task. I like to put myself on notice and get to work. I close the door and hang a *Do Not Disturb* sign letting others around me know I'm focusing.

Every month, I create a Focus Folder which include my goals, timelines, special contacts, important dates of meetings, important phone numbers, and anything else that is pertinent. I also write down strategies for building my career in sales. I learned this early on in business. When I didn't know what to do, my Focus Folder put me easily back on track. Seeing so many of my focused plans come to fruition, my Focus Folder made me a believer.

The Focus Folder is brightly colored and has a memorable title for the month, so I can easily grab it when I need it. It helps me create my monthly calendar and organize my month at a glance. It tells me what to do, who to call for my business, even guides my conversations with clarity. If I know who I'm calling that day and what I need to get done and I have it all in one place, my work is guided, and my time is used wisely.

Sometimes the most wasted time in your day is from not knowing what you are supposed to be concentrating on.

KEEP YOURSELF ON A TIMER

Set an alarm. I set separate alarms throughout the day for different tasks. You can make it a game. I've done this for years. I don't like being beaten by the clock, which motivates me to check tasks off my list. The clock beats me more times than not, but it gives me a gauge of what is or is not working. You feel greatly accomplished when you get your things checked off your list in your Focus Folder.

THE STRUGGLE TO FOCUS

Some days my focus is better than others. Have you had days where you wondered, "What did I do today? Where did my day go? Why did I waste so much time? Why wasn't I more productive?" I certainly have.

I decide not to wallow in my disappointment and, instead, to be better than I was yesterday. Every night, before I go to bed, I make a list of my 6 most important things to do for the next day. This helps me stay on task and keep it moving. It also lets me empty out my worries and tasks before I go to sleep.

I use several strategies to focus on everyday tasks. Some work better in certain circumstances, but they all help redirect me back to my center.

THINKING THINGS THROUGH

Sabrina: A. E. Mander, author of *Clearer Thinking*, said, "Thinking is a skilled work. It is not true that we are naturally endowed with the ability to think clearly and logically without learning how or without practicing." Thinking means concentrating, developing ideas, being creative, and trusting yourself. Be informed, get an understanding, gather knowledge, listen, access situations, formulate opinions, and hear all sides of the story. You have to get quiet to give your brain breathing room.

The more clearly you think, the more focused and meaningful your actions will be. It is ok when your thinking is not quite clear, but you can learn to direct it. That is the only way we become better thinkers. Nobody has all of the answers in this life. We have found that most of life is trial and error. When one thought doesn't work, we try another. The process repeats itself until there is success in our thinking.

PLANNING

Sabrina: Nothing happens without a plan. You have to plan for getting a job, graduating from college, getting married, having a baby (well, maybe you don't always plan that one), getting promoted, starting a business, and on and on. You must plan your work and *work your plan.*

For us, a plan always starts with an objective. I think about how we moved 6 times to different states in 10 years and wondered how we did it. We had plans, that's how we did it. Here's an example of what made our plans successful:

1. The objective was clear.
2. We created a blueprint for success.
3. We had a timeline to have certain tasks completed.
4. We created a team of people to help achieve the goals.
5. We executed the plan.
6. We evaluated the systems: Did they work or not?
7. We made revisions to make the plan work better.

Believe in the plan. I'm a firm believer that your belief will always overcome what you see. Even if the plan of action seems massive and out of reach, your vision, your plan, your implementation, is what will drive the project. You may be the only person that sees it or believes in the plan. Don't let that dissuade or discourage you. That belief system will get you through the doubters, disappointments, and setbacks along the way.

And just know that there will be many on your course to achieving that goal.

I've never given much credence to the naysayers of the world. Most won't understand your vision. A solid plan creates success. When I think of my plan, I think goals, team, ideas, marketing, competition, and performance. Attitude is everything. There will be days that nothing is going right, but it helps to keep your head space strong, put a smile on your face, and keep moving forward.

Do the small, achievable tasks first in the plan and keep building momentum.

Wins are wins and they matter, big or small. Focus on your focus. Eliminate distractions by first understanding what the distractions are and start at the top. Make a list, then proceed removing them one by one. Some will be harder than others, but to get where you need to be, they all must go!

Distractions are negative energy that cloud your head and drain your spirits. If you're not focused, you may miss hitting breakthroughs that will be crucial on your journey to accomplish the goal.

When creating your plan, state your objectives, explain the situation, and list your options. Always have a Plan A,

Plan B and sometimes, C. Analyze what options will work best right now and why, then decide how to execute.

STRATEGIZE

Life takes strategy. You cannot just go along to get along. You must be strategic and intentional to create success. Whether you are strategizing for a successful, safe vacation, launching a successful business, getting your child into an Ivy League school or earning an Olympic Gold medal, strategy is key!

First, set your goals and decide what actions must be taken. Decide who takes the actions. Work the numbers, explore options, compare data, and talk the strategy out with others who are critical thinkers. Surround yourself with others who are better in certain areas than you are so your expertise complements one another. Be a great listener as you bounce ideas off each other. Read to become knowledgeable on a subject and always see the big, finished product.

WRITE DOWN YOUR THOUGHTS

I write it all down. An old proverb says that the faintest ink is more powerful than the strongest memory. When a thought comes to mind, write it down. That thought leads to action. Your body does what the mind tells it to do. Your thoughts control your actions and writing it down allows you to organize those thoughts and direct them toward a goal.

CREATE GOAL POSTERS

I've grown up with goal posters my entire professional career. Being in direct sales, you must SEE it to BE it. I create an aspirational collage, using simple cutouts from magazines with images that define my lifestyle—the house, the car, the kind of people I want in my tribe. Visualization is the key to success. Now we have fancy vision boards, including everything that inspires us—from pictures to favorite quotes, favorite people, and memories. It can be any visual form that inspires you, but here's how you start a vision board.

VISION BOARD:

- Set goals and prioritize them.
- Create a basic structure for your board, such as work goals on the left and family on the right.
- Write your goals and ideas on your board.
- Find images and words that move you and add those to your board.
- Sort and arrange your board to fit your structure.
- Edit your board: Take out pieces that are not important and add more where you need it.
- Glue down your images in a visual layout that appeals to you.

Now, put your board up where you can see it and be motivated every day.

ACCOUNTABILITY PARTNERS

An accountability partner is paramount to success. In business, in marriage, in fitness, in competition, in faith... simply in our lives, we have found ourselves better when we are accountable to something or somebody. An accountability partner helps you stay on track with your focus, attention, and goals.

Over the years, Kenny and I have held each other accountable, been held accountable by others, and have held countless others accountable in our chosen coaching careers. (Kenny in athletics, Sabrina in her sales organization.)

You must *power-up with the powerful* and not *with the pitiful.* Powerful accountability partners give you firm, measurable tasks with a deadline; the pitiful allow you to stray from the tasks, create excuses, and not be a finisher. Who you are connecting with is important to get the job done. There are dreamers and doers. A great partner will do both well.

We like to refer to our best accountability partners as *power partners.* They should be uplifting, empowering, strategic, optimistic, and genuine. They should not just tell you what you want to hear; they must tell you what you *need to hear.*

They also should be a great listener. Many times, we know the answer to the question; we just need the question asked in a different voice to ponder our thoughts and think the solution through.

Life can be challenging, figuring everything out on

your own. You need someone to help guide your creativity flow; our editor did that for us in this book. Our editing sessions are not long, but they are necessary to move the book along. The agreement between you and your accountability partner will vary by project based on the time commitment, the frequency of check-ins, and how you will communicate.

Life coaches are a big business these days, evidence there is a great need for coaching, assessing, and evaluating to get to a place of centeredness and success.

PRAYER AND AFFIRMATIONS

Take God as your power partner in all aspects of life. I always ask God for focus and clarity. I pray for understanding on who to partner with, asking God to place people in my path who are likeminded. Prayer leads to clarity in your thinking, doing, and being. Another way to encourage yourself is through affirmations. Words work. One of my favorite books, "What to Say When You Talk to Yourself," by acclaimed psychologist Shad Helmstetter is a life-changing guide that helps you help yourself through motivational self-talk and positive thinking. Your **attitude** determines your **altitude**. The words you say to yourself are the most important words you will hear. You must depend on yourself to optimize your outlook and to focus your plans.

Rephrasing words can make all the difference. For example, just say, "Good God, it's morning!" or you could say "Good morning God." Positive words are empowering words, and they can help you maintain or shift your mindset.

AN OLYMPIC FEAT OF EPIC PROPORTIONS

Kenny: I believe my ability to focus on my goals and block out or eliminate distractions is one my greatest attributes. I realized at a very young age that whenever I wanted to accomplish something, whether it was in the classroom or in sports, I made great progress when I concentrated on learning and on getting better in my skillset. It became a habit, but in the beginning, it was trial and error.

I got great results when I honed in on the task at hand, which helped me understand it better, like studying my performance after a wrestling match, and that helped me start to believe in my abilities. My two older brothers were instrumental in providing leadership and examples of how to be a great team player. They helped me to understand the importance of creating a winner's circle, meaning if the team wins, I win. Once I realized how important leadership was in maximizing my potential, my focus turned to learning how to be a better leader by watching and studying leaders. I learned from my coaches, teachers, administrators, and champions. I was always a student of the game.

One of the biggest examples of the power of focus happened during one of the most important moments of my life. It was in 1992, 6 days before the opening ceremony of the 1992 Olympic Games. I had made my second Olympic Team and was prepared and very motivated to defend my 1988 Olympic Gold medal, where I had defeated the 1987 world champion from Russia in overtime. The 1992 Olympic Games in Barcelona, Spain was arguably one of the most watched Olympic Games and drew worldwide press, mainly because of the USA basketball team, "The Dream Team," featuring Michael Jordan, Charles Barkley, and others. It was a very exciting time to be on Team USA regardless of the sport you were representing.

After winning Gold in 1988 and a world title in 1989, I had two disappointing years. Not making the US world team in 1990 and losing a very close match in the finals of the world championships in 1991 caused me to get totally refocused on getting back to the level I was competing at in 1988 and 1989. I felt tremendous going into the 1992 Olympic trials, winning two straight matches in the best of three series against four-time NCAA Champion and younger brother of legendary six-time world and Olympic champ, John Smith.

It was the last training day of the week and the final practice of the day. During the last 30 seconds of our sparring match that the coaches had run the Olympic team through, my partner tried a dangerous move and collapsed his body on my left arm, hyperextending my elbow. I screamed out in pain, and the whole room got really quiet. I immediately thought it was over and that my dream of winning my second Olympic Gold was destroyed. I was rushed to the training room and then to the hospital to see how bad my injury was.

In my 30-year career in wrestling, I had never had

a severe injury. I've had cut eyes that required stitches and a few sprained ankles but nothing that felt like what I was feeling in my elbow. I was devastated. All I could think about was all the hard work that I had put in and the sacrifices I had made to be at my best. Now, I wasn't going to be able to compete.

My whole arm, from my fingers all the way up to my shoulders, was starting to swell. The head trainer for the Olympic Games came in with the doctor, and they took an X-ray of my elbow.

The doc said, "I've got good news and bad. Which would you like to hear first?"

Of course, I wanted to hear some good news after telling myself all the bad news in my head.

"The good news is there is nothing torn. All ligaments are in place, and it was just badly hyperextended. It's not going to require surgery, and if your arm wasn't so strong and in such great condition, we would be having a different conversation."

So, I then asked for the bad news. I knew he was going to say I'm out and cannot wrestle in the Olympic Games.

"Well," he said, "I'm not going to say you can't compete. But I will say it's going to be painful, and you're not going to be 100%. Let's take it day by day. Ice and stem treatments three times a day and see how it responds."

I left the doctor's office encouraged and feeling better about my chances of competing.

With only 6 days before the tournament started, my mindset shifted. Now I really had to focus on a few things. First, how was I going to continue to work out and keep my weight down without getting on the mat? Second, since I had to wear a sling to keep my arm in place, how was I going to move around Olympic Village, going to and from the cafeteria without showing my injury to my competitors? Third, my coaches and I had to devise a plan of attack. How was I going to compete strategy-wise with my elbow being hurt?

Immediately, I decided to just focus on the things I could control. I brought bikes and weights to my room so I could continue to work out without going to the practice room. I had trainers bring coolers and a microwave to my room, so I didn't have to go to the cafe as often. I really had to focus on working my legs and core exercises to stay sharp. I meditated every day and would repeat positive affirmations 4 or 5 hours a day. I focused on keeping a good attitude by telling myself and anyone that would ask, "I'm getting better. My arm is getting stronger, and the swelling is going down," even though it wasn't.

It wasn't until 24 hours before the first match of the Olympic Games that the swelling in my elbow started to subside. I was very excited at that point, because even though I knew I wasn't going to be 100%, I believed I was healthy enough to compete at a high level.

The thing that helped me to overcome the disappointment of my injury was the power of a great attitude. I just refused to let it defeat me. My focus and my belief system were instrumental in getting me ready to compete.

I had one of my best performances, winning the Silver medal and only giving up one point in seven matches!

CONCLUSION

In life, focusing on the focus helps eliminate distractions, and keeps the main thing *the main thing.* You must train your brain to focus, not to wander, and find ways to pay attention. In this difficult world, it is easy to become distracted, to start surfing social media, pick up the telephone to chit-chat, to daydream— anything other than what we are supposed to be doing. Creative avoidance can be a big problem, doing anything to avoid what needs to be done.

Accountability is the key to maintaining focus. That's why an accountability partner works for diet and exercise. There is a buddy who helps you maintain focus. In writing this book, having an editor has helped us sustain focus. If we didn't have deadlines and weekly meetups, we would not have the sense of urgency to write, to complete chapters, and to put this book together. Implement systems that keep your focus sharp and find people to hold you accountable.

Notes/Reflections

FIGHT

Kenny: My first introduction to the fight game started early in my life. At birth to be exact. My mother had a tubal ligation (tubes tied) after my two brothers were born – Michael, 6 years previously and then Jim, 4 years later. My mother, Elizabeth, tells the story of how she and my father, Fred, had decided that two boys were enough, and she didn't want to go through another pregnancy because both were difficult. My parents and the doctors were very surprised that my mother had an incomplete closing of her fallopian tube that resulted in her getting pregnant with me. The tubal ligation procedure is 99% effective, and I was the 1% that made it through! In essence, I was born to fight!

Being the youngest of three boys, I was fighting early. It began with me just fighting for respect from my older brothers. I was very determined for as long as I can remember to not be average at anything. It was always very competitive in our house, and my brothers and I competed at just about everything from football to basketball, baseball, track, and wrestling. Whatever the sports season, we were playing and trying our very best to win!

The neighborhood where I grew up in Tulsa was also very competitive. There were many two-parent families in "the Hood," the name that we gave our neighborhood which became well known all over North Tulsa. As you can see, my competitive fire was lit when I was very young, and it grew and developed into a full- grown desire to be the very best at whatever I was doing or whatever sport I played. Wrestling is first an individual sport—*mano a mano*. It's a very tough and demanding sport that requires a great deal of discipline. It's a sport where you are trained to fight for every point and to control your opponent. That fighting spirit carried over into many areas of my life.

Whenever I encountered a setback or a difficult challenge, I would always refer back to the core principles and the fundamentals I learned from the sport of wrestling. I also was taught to fight for my beliefs, the things that really mattered in my life.

WHEN YOU DON'T FIGHT, YOU LOSE

Muhammad Ali once said, "Champions are made from something they have deep inside them. A desire, a dream, a vision. They have to have last-minute stamina. They have to be a little faster. They have to have the skill and the will. But the will must be stronger than the skill."

When you don't fight for the life you deserve, you settle. You quit! You stop striving for your best. Consider your WHY when developing a fighter's mentality. You must know your why. If the why is burning deep inside your soul, you will figure it out and fight for it with all you have. The **why** is more important than the **how**. The why will make you do it anyway. The why doesn't let you quit. It drives you daily. It keeps you on the path of progress.

DEVELOPING A FIGHT MENTALITY IS CRUCIAL TO CREATING SUCCESS

We have always believed if we are backed into a corner, we are coming out swinging! Many times, in life, your best punches are thrown when you are up against the wall and had no choice. We are all born with an instinct to want to win. Some work harder at it than others.

SET HIGH EXPECTATIONS

If you don't have something to fight for that will stretch you, there is nothing to strive for. The fight in life is a standard you set for yourself. Our youngest son, Quincy, has worked to be a great student all of his school years. When it was time to make his college choice, it came down to UNC Chapel Hill, where his older brother attended and wrestled and where his dad coached, or Princeton University, the number one school in the country at the time. Both were great schools to matriculate for higher education.

Quincy decided on Princeton, the road less traveled. He thought UNC would be the easier, more comfortable choice; however, he wanted to fight for a stretch goal. He wanted to create a path of his own. Unchartered territory. He wanted to fight for his own identity.

He knew making the decision on his own would be difficult, however, fighting for independence, creating a future from an Ivy League University, would give him options and opportunities not afforded to him at UNC. We were proud of him being able to set the expectation for himself and fight for what would be the life he desired to live, living for himself and no one else. Many times, when you are fighting for your dreams, you have to dig deep, search your soul, and know you have one life to live, so live it for YOU, no matter how unpopular or uncommon it may appear.

BE RESILIENT AND CONFIDENT

Kenny: Be ready for anybody, with anything, anyhow. When you have a fighting spirit, there is also the tenacity to confront and approach any situation with no fear. You must understand chances must be taken. There are no guarantees in life. Go after the desires of your heart. Be unapologetic with your belief system. Nobody else can beat you in fighting for yourself.

When you get knocked down, you must get back up. Bounce back ability is key.

Learn the lessons and keep moving. My dad called it, *the school of hard knocks.* We both had parents who allowed us to make mistakes and learn from them.

Confidence should never be confused with arrogance. There is a difference.

Confidence is a knowing. Arrogance is a telling. When you work and walk in confidence, your actions speak louder than words. Confidence attracts people, places, and things to you.

Sabrina: When I contract out for a service, the first thing I look for is confidence. How you speak, how you look, how you know your product and its services. I want to work with people who know their craft inside and out. I don't have to wonder if that person is competent. From my hairstylist to my CPA to my housekeeper, we want to know the job is getting done without question. We work on confidence daily. Your confidence level should be consistent. When you believe in yourself, it's easier for others to believe in you.

BE COMPETITIVE

You are your greatest competition. Every day is a chance to get better, an opportunity to beat yourself. Stop comparing yourself to others. Focus on your best, that will take care of the rest. Competition is great. It is measured. It gives you a benchmark. It keeps you hungry. Embrace the competition and allow it to be a steppingstone.

A competitive spirit is a healthy way to develop enthusiasm, become a great teammate, and competitor. Our country is built on competition, and it is the spirit of the Olympics and our nation.

It helps you to learn to fight for what you want. Basic fundamentals of competition are taught in the peewee league. Competition in the classroom and in the workplace makes everybody better. We were taught early in life *you win some, you lose some..., you must dress for them all* (Satchel Paige). Competition sharpens the tools in your box. Compete is what we do.

BE DETERMINED

Think about when you have been determined to get something done. You were unstoppable. The sheer fact that you made up your mind created a certain fight in your spirit that no one could match. We must be moved in a way that reaches down into our core that gives us a Yes, I Can, No Matter What Attitude.

This reminds me of a story when a woman's baby needed shoes, but at the time, she was struggling financially. The woman never once questioned if she was going to get them, it was when? She was bound and determined to find a solution. Period, end of discussion. When one is determined, the only plan is to get it done. When one is determined, you will go over, under, around, and through!

VISUALIZE VICTORY

We mentioned before: You must SEE it to BE it. Visualization keeps us on task. You must visualize the victory. In your mind's eye, you should see the other side. What does it look like? What does it feel like? Who is with you on the victory lap? During the biggest fights of our lives, we always saw the big picture.

Kenny: When I lost to the Russian that I had faced twice before, the odds weren't in my favor. My vision of being the Olympic champ wasn't a clear path and it wasn't easy. Being able to visualize where I wanted to be has always been critical in my success. I visualize State titles, NCAA titles, World titles, Olympic titles, being inducted into National Halls of Fame... and that was just the beginning! I visualized my name being called by the announcer into the International Hall of Fame, and that became a reality for me in 2019 in Budapest, Hungary. In visualization, 5 senses are used: seeing, smelling, hearing, tasting and hearing.

In our family, we work to be strong, tough-minded fighters in this thing called life.

A fighter's spirit is engrained in who we are. We taught our children to work toward developing those same characteristics.

One of our favorite readings basically depicts the fighter's mentality: "Every morning in Africa, a gazelle wakes up. It knows it must be faster than the fastest lion or it will be killed. Every morning, a lion wakes up. It knows it must outrun the slowest gazelle or it will starve to death. It doesn't matter whether you are a lion or a gazelle.

"When the sun comes up, you'd better be running." (Christopher McDougall, Born to Run: A Hidden Tribe, Super athletes, and the Greatest Race the World Has Never Seen.)

You must fight, or you will lose. Daily, we fight for faith, family, friends, and finances. We don't expect anything to be given to us. The more we fight for what we believe we deserve, the more control and clarity we have. Don't leave your life in the hands of others. You take control. You dictate the course of your livelihood.

QUINCY WINS STATE

Kenny: While we lived in Florida, the school our youngest son, Quincy, attended did not have a wrestling team; therefore, he had to take a year off from the sport.

When we moved to Texas during his freshman year, there was one kid projected to start in front of him. The coaches were high on this kid; the teammates were high on this kid. Quincy had to fight his butt off in the practice room to earn respect. He had to put it all on the line. He had to spar his teammate daily.

At the beginning of practice, the other kid was getting the best of Quincy, but Quincy was not going to be denied the starting spot. He had to put in the extra work, go in earlier, and stay later. He had to believe in himself when others didn't. They battled in practice, and Quincy got better. He had to fight through adversity, fight against all odds and close the gap in a relatively short timeframe. Fighting through obstacles at practice paid dividends for Quincy his first year of high school coming in from another state. He ended up earning the starting position and winning his first state title. He went on to become a 4-time high school state champion like his dad.

EMBODYING OUR LEGACY

Kenny: One of my earliest examples of learning and understanding the significance of fight mentality came from my parents. When I was entering my freshman year of high school, 9th graders were not eligible to compete on the high school level. Even though my high school had a freshmen class, only the 10th through 12th grades could participate in varsity athletics. My parents knew how bad I wanted to make the varsity team and have an opportunity to be the first 4x state champion in the state of Oklahoma. They went to countless school board meetings and gathered hundreds of petition signatures to plead my case. They eventually won and the school board voted to allow freshmen to compete on varsity athletic teams for the first time. That tenacity and never-give-up attitude stayed with me for the rest of my life and showed how important it was to fight for your family, even against all odds.

My wife and I use the same mentality when it came time to fight for our kids' education. We brought our three kids up in public schools, which sometimes can be very challenging, working with teachers and administrators where there was a high ratio of kids per teacher. My wife spent many hours up at the schools throughout our kids' early education being a teacher's aide and supporting the administration in any gaps that were present.

I can recall when our daughter, Sydnee, was trying out for the cheer squad.

Cheerleading has changed from the times of just pom poms and smiles. These girls and guys needed to know how to tumble and do round-offs to make the team. It was a challenging experience because our daughter had to work hard to develop her tumbling skills. She wanted to make the cheer squad but wasn't sure she could develop the skills necessary to make the team. We decided to hire a private gymnast to work with her so she would be ready and prepared for the tryouts. It was a tough couple of months, and sometimes she thought about quitting, but we stressed the importance of fighting through the tough times and working hard to overcome the setbacks and disappointments. She stayed with it and began to learn the skills necessary to make the team. The trials were a week away and she was ready. She made the team and became one of the cheer captains her senior year.

It turned out to be a good experience and she was thankful that she fought through the tough times and achieved one of her goals. The lesson in this is even when things look impossible or if you think you're not good enough, if you believe in yourself and fight for what you believe in, and work hard, you can be successful.

HAVE ENERGY TO FIGHT – MASTER THE MIND

Kenny: As you can see from both of our children's examples, fighting takes effort. You have to keep showing up in the lab of life. Practice makes perfect. You cannot get tired in the middle of the fight.

Having a fighting spirit requires stamina and that includes eating right. Here are some energy-boosting superfoods that give you all day power:

1. Cottage cheese
2. Salmon
3. Steel cut oats
4. Greek yogurt
5. Almonds
6. Roasted chickpeas
7. Tuna with whole wheat crackers

8. Matcha

9. Dark chocolate

10. Whole wheat bread with ricotta

11. Avocado

12. Eggs

13. Sweet potatoes

14. Quinoa

15. Walnuts

16. High fiber cereal with milk

17. Spinach

18. Lentils

19. Bananas

20. Homemade trail mix

21. Melon

22. Lots of water; drinking One Gallon a Day Keeps the Doctor Away.

To fight our best fight, we must fuel the engine to run at an optimal level. Every day, we are challenged to eat right; do not forget to keep the fight in the forefront.

Core exercises like cardio – a simple walk of 15-20 minutes a day, clears the head and gets the body moving. Endorphins are released, and you have better head space to fight the good fight. Exercise especially boosts cardiovascular health and fitness and improves the body's ability to circulate oxygen. This improves energy immediately, but over time, you also feel less tired when in better physical condition. Normal, daily tasks are easier and less draining when you are physically fit. Exercises that boost your energy are breath work, a brisk walk, yoga, jump roping, and dancing.

Sleeping well is another must for a healthy disposition. We understand the power of great rest. Sleep is needed for a number of reasons, including energy conservation, restoration of our tissues and cognitive function, emotion regulation, and immune health. The body has multiple systems regulating our sleep/wake cycle and our journey through the cycle of sleep stages. These processes work together to ensure we get deep, restful sleep and have energy throughout the day.

Be good to your body for superior performance. A fighter is built to last. A fighting mentality goes the distance. You are always training for a challenge, as in life, there will always be obstacles to overcome. A fighter doesn't shy away from the hard things in life, but you train through it. This applies to business, life, relationships, sports and in the long run, the greatest challenges have made us better.

You must continually be in training mode. The best of the best is *always* in school. Many times, the teacher who is teaching learns the greatest lessons. What you send into the lives of others comes back into your own. We often get out of life what we put in. Every time I'm asked to speak, train, teach, in preparing for the presentation, I get better. When I teach, I'm my best student. I'm reminded to apply the many years of training and education that I used previously over the years to help me reignite the fire within.

Notes/Reflections

Monday Family
Early Days

Sabrina Monday and her daughter Sydnee, 2, show their American flags as they prepare Friday, July 12, 1996, to leave from their Tulsa home for the Olympics in Atlanta. STEPHEN PINGRY / Tulsa World file

FORTITUDE

Kenny: We define fortitude in our lives as being courageous and having a strong mentality. One of the pivotal times of my life was in 1986 and 1987. I was in training with high hopes of making the Olympic Team in 1988. At the time, I was third ranked on the USA National Team. The two wrestlers in front of me—and the biggest threats to keep me off that 1988 Olympic Team—were two of the best wrestlers in the world. One was Nate Carr, 3-time NCAA Champion, who had beat me in two of those NCAA finals, and the defending Olympic Champ in LA 1984 and world champ in 1983, Dave Schultz.

I had beat Carr a few times, but I had yet to beat Schultz after three attempts at that point. So going into the Olympic trials in 1988, I was a huge underdog and very few people, if any, were picking me to win. I was really working hard and getting better, but not at the rate I wanted or needed. I had an extremely high mountain to climb. I never got discouraged, but I was a bit frustrated that I wasn't closing that gap as quickly as I'd have liked. Time was moving fast, and I was starting to feel the pressure.

After a very hard 4-week training cycle, I had scheduled a 5-day rest and recovery period to let my mind and body get refreshed. During that break, I got invited to help at the Special Olympic Games, which was being held at home, in Stillwater, OK. It was fun, working with the volunteers and all of the S.O. athletes were amazing. All the Special Olympic athletes that participated were excited to be a part of the games. They all tried extremely hard and gave their best effort. There were definitely more hugs than medals given out that day, and they were appreciative of our time. I left there that day incredibly humbled and with a new sense of purpose. I knew I needed to adjust my mindset.

I was putting too much pressure on myself and wasn't clear in my vision. After that experience with the Special Olympics, I decided to just enjoy the process. I was blessed to have a sound mind and body to compete in the sport I loved with an opportunity to make the Olympic Team. It wasn't going to be easy, but from that point on, I just focused on being courageous and giving the journey the very best I had and not worry about losing. I started making amazing gains on daily basis, and my vision was clear and sharp.

GO GET IT

Success in life will not just come to you; you must go get it. There will be times when things get tough, whether it be physically, mentally, or financially— obstacles that will occur that you cannot control. Whether you fight or flee is a choice. It takes great fortitude to stand your ground and reach for success.

Fortitude is the willingness to act in spite of fear, to be steadfast in your life's pursuit. Don't be easily shaken and thrown off course. We have heard this old adage for years and we should adhere to it: "When the going gets tough, the tough get going."

Fortitude helps us avoid settling in life. It helps us avoid negativity, doubt, naysayers, and helps me fight my way through the pitfalls. Without fortitude in my life, I wouldn't be the man I am and I wouldn't be the coach I am if I hadn't had it to push through the challenges of life.

DEVELOPING FORTITUDE

Kenny: Fortitude can be learned through the stories of others who have fought through situations and persevered. It is empowering to watch athletes come from behind and win. As you watch others overcome adversity, you become inspired. Tennis great Serena Williams is a champion who epitomizes fortitude. How often have we seen her down two sets and come back victorious? Staying focused, working with a strategy, managing your emotions, and believing in your best creates a winning mentality. Embracing the process, not cutting corners, putting in the work—*working not wishing*—will always give you favorable results.

Fortitude will help you move through life's difficulties, whether they be injuries, the loss of victories, the loss of family and friends, difficult relationships, setbacks, or distractions. Grit, grace, and grind along the way have helped create the strong path for success. Life is met with many peaks and valleys; how we navigate the highways, the forks in the road, increases our fortitude daily, helps us be better, and be forever overcomers.

When you lean in and learn to stare adversity in the face, you become a distance runner in life. You decide that going the distance is the only way out. This discipline takes you further than the next person. Without fortitude, it's easy to get off track, wander aimlessly, and accept defeat. We have found that there are those in life who wonder what happened, those who didn't know it happened, and those who make it happen. Those who make it happen live with the largest dose of fortitude in their lives.

Be encouraged and keep trying. Try with *umph* is Triumph. Fall forward. Surround yourself with like-minded people who are positive, passionate, courageous, and faithful. Create an environment that is conducive to winning. Train the brain to be competitive, be determined, and have relentless optimism.

During my competitive years, it was important for me to be highly competitive in the practice room. I needed to put 100% in at practice to prepare me for my matches.

My daily goal was to outwork everyone in the room, stay positive, have a great attitude, and have short- term memory on the days that were not great. On the days that I didn't have a great practice, my thought was to always be better than the day before. On the tough days, I did more sprints, more push-ups, something that would make me feel better about my time at practice. I did my best to not allow my bad days to bring me down, and I focused on getting better. The small wins add up, building toughness and confidence for tomorrow.

In all areas of life, fortitude got us through many challenges: setbacks, losing NCAA championships, parents divorcing, keeping a solid marriage for 30 plus years, the death of parents—the list goes on and on. Keep fighting for your dreams, your legacy, the many things you want to accomplish in life. They will elude you if you don't see your way through by making promises to yourself to never give up on your dreams, goals, and pursuits.

When thoughts of giving up creep into my soul, I quickly delve into my faith-filled spirit, go to my written goals, remember my why, my family support, the friends and peers who believe in me, tap into the power source, my toolbox, and find the strength to move forward. You must dig deep and find the strength you never knew you had. You are stronger than you think in most situations.

Sabrina has always loved the quote by Eleanor Roosevelt, "A woman is like a tea bag, you never know how strong it is until it's in hot water." Embrace the hot water and learn how strong you can become.

UNVEILING THE DEEPER
MEANING OF FORTITUDE

Sabrina and Kenny: Whenever you think of the word Fortitude, we want you to remember that each letter stands for something valuable. We use a simple pneumonic below to break down our vision of fortitude.

F: Figure it out

We were all born with an innate ability to solve problems. Your way may be different from mine, but you must find a way through your problems that works for you. Be confident in your thought process to come up with solutions, then solve the problem.

I remember being so very excited about the birth of our first-born daughter, Sydnee Simone Monday, born June 20, 1994, on a Monday afternoon at Hillcrest Hospital in Tulsa, Oklahoma—the same city, Kenny and I were born in. As a first-time mom, I was excited and nervous. Babies do not come with a handbook. I had read many parenting books before her delivery, and many moms gave me motherly advice; however, it's nothing like the real thing.

Nobody can tell you how your baby will or will not breastfeed. Of course, there are books, tips, and tricks on the baby latching onto the breast; however, sometimes, the experience is different for everybody. The process was difficult for me. Two different lactation specialists visited me in the hospital; I guess I was a special case. I was close to giving up, yet I was determined. The process was exhausting. It seemed all Sydnee wanted to do was eat. My milk was not producing fast enough. I felt like a failure. My doctor, during my pregnancy, had reiterated that mother's milk was best for the baby. I heard they were stronger, faster, smarter, when breastfed. All I could think of was how I was failing my kid.

After much determination, many sleepless nights, we finally got it right. Practice made perfect. I was able to nurse Sydnee for almost a year. We tried many different techniques—not always what the book said—and eventually arrived at the strategy that worked for us—the angle, the right pillow, drinking plenty of fluids, the right creams to ease the pain. The doctor and lactation specialist advised me, however, in the end, mama and baby had to figure it out.

Life is like that. It takes effort, experience, trial and

error to figure things out. You must be capable, willing, and able, but most of all, you must have the patience and perseverance to figure it out.

O: Options and opportunities

If God brought us to it, we believe God will bring us through it. We see and seek the many wondrous possibilities because we believe in a world of limitless ideas. The only limits that exist are self-imposed. Be aware of your options and embrace opportunities as they appear.

When our son, Quincy, was playing little league Pop Warner football at age 10, the starting quarterback on our team was a good athlete, but he couldn't remember the plays. He kept forgetting them. The coach became increasingly frustrated and started looking for someone that could replace the quarterback. Quincy, at the time, had been practicing both positions at home. We told him he needed to learn both positions to be prepared; he never knew what position he might have to play. The coach became totally frustrated. One practice, he said, "I just need somebody to remember the plays." Quincy raised his hand and eagerly volunteered. The coach gave

Quincy 4 plays to run one time, and Quincy remembered all of them. He became the starting quarterback the rest of the season. Preparation meets opportunity. Sabrina's dad always said that, "You should stay ready so you don't have to get ready."

R: Risks

Stop being safe. Some of your greatest rewards come when you take the greatest risks. You are stretched when you get out of your comfort zone. Take the risk or lose the chance but also *embrace the chance to lose.* If you win, you will be happy; if you lose, you will be wise!

In our 30 years of marriage, our family has moved 6 times. Kenny is a coach, so we tend to move where the winning is (or where he needs to create it). We have made the adjustments to new schools, new neighborhoods, new churches, new friends, and new workspaces. Every single move was a risk; there were no guarantees. Yes, there are always concerns: Is this the right move? Will we be successful? Will the children be happy? Again, if God brings us to it, He will bring us through it. You have to trust the process and lean on your faith.

Muhammad Ali quoted, "He who is not courageous enough to take risks will accomplish nothing in life." Be bodacious, courageous, and audacious in your **Be**ing and **Do**ing.

T: Talk

Talk to yourself in a way that is positive, that builds you up. Stop self-sabotage.

What you say to yourself is important to your health and well-being. We live in a negative world. Society, many times, tells us what we are not, what we can't be. You must be your greatest fan, the biggest advocate of who and what you are becoming, in spite of the challenges you face.

Many times, we are our greatest enemy. If you think about it, your words are the first words you hear in your mind. You think them before you speak them. Experts estimate that the mind thinks between 60,000 and 80,000 thoughts a day. That's an average of 2,500– 3,300 thoughts per hour. Other experts estimate a smaller number— 50,000 thoughts per day, which still means about 2,100 thoughts per hour. (successconsciousness.

com.) These numbers are incredible. The mind races; that's just what it does. But it's important to think about what you are thinking and how you are thinking.

The brain can be trained. Who and what are you listening to? When you take garbage in, garbage is certainly what will come out. Be intentional with what you are feeding your mind subconsciously. The words you say to yourself make a difference.

Affirmations throughout the day are just a reminder of who you are becoming. Most people fail because of low self-esteem and a lack of self-confidence. It is imperative to think positive thoughts and speak positive words over your life.

These short statements can make a difference in your life when spoken daily:

- I love myself.
- I am a great work in progress.
- I am a magnet for success.
- I am enough.

There is an app called **I AM** that sends you positive affirmation alarms throughout the day. Tools like this will help you remember to speak positively into your life. BE intentional on formulating positive thoughts into the brain. Negativity breeds negativity. Negative words are as powerful as positive words.

I'm lazy. I'm dumb. I'm a failure. These words bring you down and strip you of confidence and wellbeing. Pay attention to the words you speak and the words you allow others to speak about you. In rearing our children, we did our best to make sure our home was filled with positive, uplifting words that were encouraging. Your words do matter. Our two boys started wrestling at five and six years old and competed throughout college at division one schools. There were many years of competition when there were losses, but we didn't focus on all that went wrong or dwell on the disappointment. We taught the many lessons of winning in losing. We asked them to note how they got better from the experience, and they learned to learn from failure.

I: Integrity

Integrity is always being who you are when no one is watching. Live with a spirit of good will. Live with the notion of getting better every day. Live knowing many around you will want to emulate you in one way or another—the way you treat others, your humble spirit, your ability to push past your present situation. Integrity is living a life that is noble, not for show and tell, but for the good of others and having a servant's heart.

Integrity means you live in accordance with your deepest values, being honest with yourself and everyone around you. Your word is your bond. I have led a sales force of thousands of people for 30 plus years. These people trust me with their leadership. If I didn't work my business with integrity, I would not be valued as a leader. It is impossible to lead others for long periods of time without integrity. There would be no trust, no value, and no success. With leadership, there must be follow-ship.

Without integrity, you would be compromising the essence of your soul. A trusted leader possesses integrity, one of the most important traits individuals should strive for in life. When you are open, honest, and have a good reputation, you feel at peace; you are confident in who you are, and you have good relationships because you are authentically yourself. There is nothing to hide. You become admirable, you inspire others, and you lead by example. It is difficult to lead others to greatness when the pillar of integrity is missing.

T: Talent

Talent resides in each of us that we many times don't tap into. Identify your many gifts. What do you like to do and what are you good at? Spend time investing in your gifts, growing them, and sharing them with others.

In rearing our children, we dug deep to find their gifts. The only way the gifts were found, though, is through exposure. We exposed them to song, dance, music, and sports. We wanted them to be well-rounded. We knew they wouldn't like it all, but we had to see what they gravitated to most. We put our children in music, and the boys gravitated toward the saxophone. They were really good, reaching first chair on many occasions. They both took to this instrument with ease. Our daughter took guitar lessons, and she took that affection of the guitar with her into her college and her young adult days.

From swimming to track, to musical instruments, to modeling lessons, we explored everything we could with them. We tried it all. There were some things they had no real interest in, and that's okay. You will find your fit when you explore and develop a fondness for certain activities. You will begin to resonate with a specialty or calling and will find you have a passion for it. Family genetics, following a sibling, or other family influences can also attribute in helping you identify your talent.

Many people struggle with finding their gifts. Their special qualities and talents may not seem of great importance. If you have an instinct or are drawn to a hobby, sport, musical instrument, or an area of your work, pursue the interest. You never know where that passion can take you.

Spend time with what interests you and build on the skill. Many have talents that are untapped because we don't take the necessary time to identify and develop the talent that resides within us. Your gifts will make room for you. Invest the time, energy, and effort in your craft. You don't get better by sitting on your gifts; you must activate them. Give your gifts away and share with the world.

Once you identify your talents, put them to work by exploring and building your life around them. Who you are, what you do, how you show up and share with the world matters. You have a lot to give, so GIVE IT. The world needs you and your talent.

U: Understanding

Understand that life is never without adversity. Life is not what happens to us; however, it is how we respond to our life's happenings. Always look to be the victor and not the victim. Life's lessons make us wiser and stronger.

Knowing and understanding are related concepts, but they are not the same. Understanding is a tool. It helps people assimilate new information and continually refine their world by seeing connections. Understanding is necessary to evaluate new information. Always be available to see new things, create new levels of knowledge that you can better comprehend. As we are challenged in our daily lives to live our best lives, it's the understanding of oneself, others, and situations that gives you the breadth and depth to embrace life's lessons and learn from them.

D: Decide

You must decide to take life and give it all that you have. Don't just accept what life gives you. You have the choice to change your situation. Take action and move life in a different direction. Create a different scenario and create a circle of influence that will help you dictate your life's outcome.

Kenny: I took a job out of college at Arizona State University to be coached by one of the best coaches in the world, Bobby Douglass. He was the first African American to coach a team to the NCAA wrestling team title in 1985. I thought I would thrive in that situation; however, I wasn't getting what I needed in that environment. I didn't have the workout partners, and I felt I wasn't making the progress I needed to make it. I was there two and a half years and had to make the decision to stay or leave. It was difficult.

I made the hard decision like those I had earlier made in my wrestling career. I decided to leave and go back to Oklahoma State University in 1987. The Olympic trials were approaching in one year, and I knew I had to get better training partners and establish a training environment where I felt I could get better. As difficult as the decision was, it was one of my best. Moving back to my home state where I had a better support system, my training got better, and I made progress. I put the work in. I was able to make the 1988 Olympic Team. One decision can change the trajectory of your life forever.

E: Endure

We must all endure the hardships of life, learn the lessons, become wiser and stronger. Take inventory of how you must get stronger. School is never out for the Pro. Life should be forever evolving. At every stage of life, there should be new-found energy, education, excitement, and less ego. Stop letting your ego get in the way of becoming better.

Life has certainly not been easy for us. Quite honestly, the more success you attain, the bigger the obstacles you will have to overcome. When times have been most challenging for us, we have had to rely on our fundamental beliefs. With God as our Alpha and Omega, we know from whom all blessings flow. We know that prayer changes things. We have learned things are never as bad as they seem. There is always a light at the end of the tunnel. Never give up on yourself.

Stay grounded. Remind yourself to stay in the present. Control what you can control, and let the rest go. Work to build a body of thick skin. Life is going to happen, you will make mistakes, and you need to learn how to recover from them. Forgive yourself and forgive others. Stay positive and look for the solution to the problem. If you don't have the solution, seek somebody who does—a family member, a friend, your pastor, a therapist. The solution does exist. Don't stay in the problem.

A positive mindset will always help you overcome adversity. We all get down on ourselves at times. The key is not to stay down. This scripture has always given us hope during tough times to endure: "Then the way you live will always honor and please the Lord, and your lives will produce every kind of good fruit. All the while, you will grow as you learn to know God better and better. We also pray that you will be strengthened with all his glorious power so you will have all the endurance and patience you need. May you be filled with joy." (Colossians 1:10-11).

Kenny: Let's make fortitude a main ingredient in our DNA. That trait is contagious. When you are around it, you want it. If you don't have it, you desire it. All champions possess it. I drew strength and determination as a kid from watching Muhammad Ali overcome. Ali was ridiculed, looked down upon, and had his titles stripped from him because he refused to go to the Vietnam War. Watching him come back and become one of the greatest boxers ever was awe inspiring.

Fortitude is also bigger than you are. You never know who is watching you and drawing strength from your life story. I drew strength from others and want others to draw strength from my example.

Sabrina: Early in my sales career, I was learning the business, seeing success, and wanted to earn my first car with the company. I had built a solid customer base, and I had started to team build. My confidence was growing, however, I attempted two times to earn the first car—a red Pontiac. I came close but failed. At that point, my confidence was dwindling, and I started to question myself, thinking maybe direct sales was not for me. I had a talk with my mentor, Gloria; she was encouraging, and explained to me that I was closer than I thought, that the goal was attainable, and I just needed to change the date.

On my third attempt, I was successful. My sales and my team building all came together. I went on to earn my first car, which was a 1990 brand new Pontiac Grand Am. I was excited. Now, I am driving my 16th pink Cadillac.

Yes, every two to three years, I have been awarded a brand new car because of my business success. I'm grateful that I had a mentor who empowered me to not give up. (See disclaimer in the back of the book.)

My greatest lesson in fortitude was when I pledged Delta Sigma Theta, Alpha Chi Chapter, at Tennessee State University my sophomore year. In my young life, pledging to become a Delta on a line of 22 was downright difficult. We were named the 22 Tipping Yak Yaks because our big sisters said we talked a lot. The more we talked, the more trouble we found ourselves in.

We have a famous Delta sculpture named "Fortitude," symbolizing the attributes of strength, courage, hope, wisdom, beauty, and femininity as depicted by the 22 founders of Delta Sigma Theta Sorority Inc, founded in 1922. Those attributes have helped shape my being.

This philosophy has been passed onto family members and business associates. I did consider giving up. During the pledging process, I wasn't sure if the late nights, creating the sisterly bond, the taunting, the early mornings, balancing the pledge period and schoolwork was all worth it. But it absolutely was.

It was then I had to dig deep to find the fortitude.

When I wasn't believing in myself or the pledging process, I held on to others' beliefs around me, like my big sister Sabrina Peters. She was the big sister who whispered in my ear to fight, to believe in the bigger picture. My family members were very supportive, too. When I look back, the challenge was to see how mentally tough I was and if I could overcome the obstacles thrown my way.

Early on, I was able to count on people who saw the best in me. In my career, I was blessed by the best, Gloria Mayfield Banks, my personal recruiter and mentor, earning over $13 million in her career, always cheering me on to greatness and passing knowledge to become the best version of myself. I've watched Gloria, at the most challenging times of her life, put a smile on her face, lead with integrity, grace and grit, not allowing her circumstances to mark her as a victim, but a victor.

When you are self-employed, you better find the fortitude. If you don't work, you don't eat. I'm moved by my boys, who wrestle. They were both state champions in high school and had great college careers at UNC Chapel Hill and Princeton University.

Wrestling is a tough sport, a lot to manage—their weight while building muscle, their mind to figure out what move is coming and what move to make. They have wrestled since they were little boys; fortitude must be in their DNA. I marvel at their ability to get on that mat and play full out, win, lose, or draw. Wrestling is a single person sport, and only individual fortitude will lead to victory. There is nothing like accepting full responsibility for your wins and losses.

Notes/Reflections

FAMILY

Sabrina: It's a fact that your family relationships and how you manage them can have a big impact on your success and or failure. Family stands over everything. I grew up in a family full of love. I had 2 older brothers: Eric, 5 years older, Greg, 4 years older, and 1 younger sister, Regina; we are 13 months apart. I was the 3rd born.

My oldest brother was killed in a tragic car accident and lost his life at 31 years of age. Eric was the kindest, most handsome guy in the world. I miss him every day. I always wonder what life would be like if he were still here on Earth. Life can be short, and we don't know the day or hour when our lives will end, so we must make every day count. My brother, Greg, is a retired educator, and is also the founder of Mentoring Viable Prospects, affording inner-city youth in Atlanta the opportunity to play baseball and pursue a college education. My sister, Regina, is a member of the House of Representatives, representing District 73 in Tulsa. Her tireless, selfless work in the community comes from deep roots.

We come from a family of fighters. Growing up in Tulsa, Oklahoma, where the 1921 race massacre occurred. Firebombs were dropped, destroying an entire community, where our great grandparents' home and businesses were burned to the ground. Our grandfather was the youngest entrepreneur on Greenwood's Wall Street.

He owned a haberdashery. Everything was lost, and our family later rebuilt, owning the oldest Black newspaper in Oklahoma, the *Oklahoma Eagle*, that is still in print at over 100 years old. Our dad, Ed Goodwin Jr., helped run the newspaper before his passing in July 2013. Our 84-year-old Uncle Jim Goodwin manages it now, while still practicing law. Our grandfather, E.L. Goodwin Sr., went to law school at 50 years old. He was the first Black graduate at Tulsa University Law School. I feel blessed that my ancestors sacrificed much so that we could have this life of choices, and I do not take them lightly.

I was raised by a phenomenal woman. Our mom was sweet and spicy when needed and when necessary.

She loved her children fiercely and unconditionally. She wanted nothing but the best for each of us. She had the ability to make each of her children believe we were her favorite. She was an intelligent woman who married early and had her first of four children right out of high school.

Our father, one of the most brilliant minds I've ever met, graduated from high school at 16 and went to college. I get my entrepreneurial zest from him. He never met a stranger. Unfortunately, for much of his life, he battled alcoholism. That stripped him of all that he could have become. His alcoholism affected all members of our family. The days of drunkenness created turmoil and uncertainty in our household. One day, our dad decided that enough was enough. After many years of treatment programs and jail time for too many DUIs, he decided he was tired of that life, and he never took another drink.

That was years after our parents divorced (my freshman year in high school), and I was grown. Our Dad went on to marry 4 more different times. Our mom never remarried. Despite all they had gone through, our mom and dad remained friendly, and we felt much love and encouragement in our home. Our mom held it down when our dad could not. We didn't have a lot, but we had enough. I always said that if I could be one third of the mom to my kids that my mom was to me, I'd be doing great.

She was an amazing cook; the entire community knew that when Queet, (as we affectionately called her) cooked, everybody was eating. Her specialty homemade rolls and macaroni and cheese are still the talk of the town. Talking about cooking with love, that was our mom. Mama was a cancer survivor; however, we lost her on December 8, 2015 to related health issues. It's still hard doing life without her. She was my very best friend.

Kenny: The family is one of – if not the–most important structure in a person's life. My immediate family, including my father, mother, and two older brothers, Mike and Jim, were instrumental in helping me to become the family man I am today.

Being the youngest in the family – the "baby boy" as I am still lovingly called by my mother sometimes – had its advantages and disadvantages. I grew up four years younger than my brother, Jim, and six years younger than my eldest brother. Even though our family was close, going on annual vacations and spending a lot of time going to our sporting events, there was a gap in age between my brothers, so they were not really my playmates. We would have a good time at home playing games and wrestling around, but I was left behind a lot when they went out with friends their own age. The advantage I received from that situation is that it helped me to be more creative with my imagination. It also helped me to watch and learn from my brothers. I watched them closely, modeling their good habits and learning from their mistakes.

Growing up with a very supportive family made a huge impact on my life, helping me to believe in myself and go full steam towards my goals. One of my early wrestling coaches taught our team the value of not just being a teammate but a *great* teammate. That's when I learned that it's not just your immediate blood family that is crucial to your success, but the extended family—coaches, teammates, parents, and the families of teammates that make such an incredible difference in the life of a child. The efforts of the inner circle of families build trust and a safe environment that kids can thrive in. It also builds bridges and fills gaps when parents can't be there. We grew up with the old African proverb, "It takes a village to raise a child." That concept was central to my family, and Sabrina and I continue to live by it.

We had a few kids on our kids' wrestling team whose parents weren't around, so my mom and dad picked up the slack. They fed them, took them to practice, and to tournaments. My parents believed in all kids from our Hood. We would offer to pick kids up and buy them uniforms. As a kid, you sometimes didn't understand why your parents went the extra mile for others, but now I know it's important to give when you can, how you can, with whatever you can. Supporting those kids gave them hope and confidence and helped them go further in life. My Mama was amazing. She wrote letters of recommendation and filled out school applications; she did so much to help so many.

Lots of kids gained from my parents' help – getting them into college, helping find scholarships, and financial aid. Family is not always blood, but it is always love.

Sabrina: We cherish and value family time. Of course, like every family, we all have our issues. However, overall, we believe family comes first. Kenny and I both say our greatest achievements and our greatest challenges have been parenting our three children. Sydnee

Symone, a Howard University grad, now working for one of the largest book publishers in the world, editing children's books. Kennedy, a UNC Chapel Hill grad, personal training at the YMCA in Baltimore, and our youngest son, Quincy, a grad of Princeton University, is an assistant wrestling coach at Princeton University and is training to compete for the Paris Olympics. We are so very proud of the young adults they have become.

OTHER PEOPLE'S OPINIONS

Kenny: Family can be complicated. Maneuvering through family drama and knowing when to distance yourself from those you love most is hard. When securing goals and objectives in life is one's priority, sometimes you have to do the hard things in life to let go of OPP – Other People's Opinions! Sometimes, those who can't see your vision, including family and friends, will hold you back from success.

When I told my father I wanted to try out for the Olympic team, he didn't support the idea. He wanted me to finish college. I told him I couldn't do both – travel overseas, train, and be committed to my studies. My Dad thought I wasn't good enough yet, and I wasn't, but I was willing to go get better. If I would have listened to him, I would not have made my first Olympic team.

The odds were against me. I wasn't the favorite guy at the weight class going into the Olympic competition. However, my dream was bigger for myself than what others could see. Sometimes you have to change before others see the change. Results will always change other people's perspectives, but the number one perspective is how you see yourself.

You must be confident and strong enough to take ownership of your life, even when not popular with your loved ones. No one should believe in you more than you believe in yourself. Not your parents, siblings, or friends. My dad came around after I made the decision to do what I believed was best for my life. He began to see my commitment and my lifestyle change was necessary to create the desired growth for myself.

I understood that my vision for my life wasn't the same as everyone else. Sometimes family can put more pressure on you than they realize. When I was training, I couldn't come home for the holidays, and I missed family vacations. To them, I was being selfish, but to me, I couldn't be distracted. It was hard to get my family to understand that missing one day of training was a BIG deal. I'm grateful that my family gave me grace and room to grow to pursue my dreams.

IT'S NOT ABOUT YOU ANYMORE

Kenny: Even though you must believe in yourself and decide when to pursue your dreams, you must also realize that yours aren't the only dreams that matter. As I got older, started my own family, I realized to build a strong family unit, sacrifices must be made. Plan to give more than you take. Sometimes you must overlook your own needs for needs of the family. It should always be Family First. Life changes when children come. You are no longer the priority. It's always about their needs – as simple as watching a football game to taking them to their practice and staying after to help them get better.

At times, you may have to give up your own ambitions to foster your children's ambitions. I passed up coaching opportunities and coaching somebody else's kids because I wanted to be home and have a less hectic travel schedule to coach my own kids.

One of the greatest advantages I have benefitted from was designing my professional career in a way that allowed me the flexibility to be home and lend the support needed to my kids in school and their extracurricular activities. My wife and I very seldom missed a school function, football game, or wrestling match. Whether they were receiving an academic award or running a touchdown on the football field, to winning a wrestling tournament, we were there to cheer them on. We were also there when things didn't go their way to lift them up, go get some ice cream, and reassure them that they would do better next time.

I could always recognize the kids who had the most support in their lives. They performed at a higher level than the kids that had less support. This involvement gave our children immediate feedback and allowed us the opportunity to praise them when it was well deserved and to give constructive correction when it was needed. I could see the difference in the kids' confidence knowing we were coming to their events.

I remember one time, in particular, when the boys were in middle school, they both were on the wrestling team and in the school band where they played the saxophone, both occupying the first chair. On this cold winter night in November, we had a conflict in their schedule. The boys had a wrestling match and a band concert on the same night. This was also during the time when my wife and I had made the decision to live in two different states.

No, we were not separated because we were having problems in our marriage; I had taken a job with Oklahoma State University on their wrestling staff. My wife and daughter stayed back in Texas, so our oldest child, Sydnee, could finish high school a year early because she had accumulated enough hours. In order to finish, she needed to stay back rather than move to Oklahoma to another school.

I had to make sure the boys were prepared for their wrestling matches and also be prepared to have great band performances. It's a good thing that both activities were held in the same building not far from each other. It was my job to make sure they had their band clothes ready so as soon as the matches ended, I could get them showered and dressed to go straight to the school auditorium for the band's performance. The boys had incredible performances that night, first winning their wrestling matches, then going to play in their band's concert. The environments could not have been more opposite.

We did our best to be present for our children with all they were involved with, and this made us closer as a family. It was also helpful to the kids to teach them how to navigate combining academics and sports, which isn't always an easy balancing act. We encouraged them to be multifaceted and focused, always putting forth their best efforts.

BUILDING FAMILY SUPPORT

Here are some ways to build family support.

Share Appreciation

Show your family members you care about them. We have a family text chat. We celebrate birthdays, promotions, funny memes, and things that bring smiles to our faces. Sending love emojis often lets your family members know you are thinking about them in positive ways.

Sharing affection and showing love are crucial parts of a strong family. I have learned that not everybody is naturally affectionate—especially men. Don't let society make you believe a sensitive, compassionate man, is a sign of weakness; it shows strength. Hugs and kisses are plentiful in our household.

Celebrating victories and being supportive when someone is having a hard time is also crucial to reinforcing family bonds. Make sure the language in the house is not negative but positive. The big world we live in can easily swallow you up, and we wanted home to be a place of encouragement. Learn as a family how to cope with difficulties and crises by supporting each other and encouraging resilience. Be mindful of how others in the family are feeling when life is stressful. Work through hard situations. Share coping skills. If one family member hurts, we all hurt.

Quality Family Time

Sabrina and Kenny: We work to take vacations annually. Building those lifelong memories have been important for us. Get Away! Get in an environment that is relaxing and inspires you to make the moments matter.

For years, our annual trip was to Cabo, Mexico. It was imperative to relax and refresh as a family. The bonding time was critical to our family's success. Eminent light, love, laughter, and lessons are at the forefront of our family structure.

Family affairs strengthen the family ties. My maternal grandparents held an annual July 4th family reunion for years. It was the yearly family blast in Cherryvale, Kansas, at the family homestead, approximately 90 minutes from our hometown of Tulsa. Kenny and I have been blessed to keep the family tradition alive by hosting our last two family reunions: one in Stillwater, Oklahoma, where we once resided, and again in the summer of 2019, in Chapel Hill, North Carolina. We enjoy hosting our 80 plus family members in our home city. It is important for the older and younger generations to know one another and learn the family history. Our greatest desire is to leave a strong legacy, as we have been left. You must know where you come from to know where you are going.

Healthy Communication

Sabrina: Say what you mean and mean what you say. Promote emotionally safe and direct communication between one another. Express unwavering support, but also remember that honesty is not being afraid to tell the truth. Sparing feelings is sometimes not easy, but honesty will almost always lead to the best outcome.

I was told at a young age we were given two ears and one mouth for a reason.

We must practice less talking and more listening. People want to be heard. Take time to hear what's happening in each family member's life. Don't talk too much or be the one always offering unsolicited advice or at some point, your voice will stop being heard.

Healthy communication is important in building and maintaining healthy relationships. Over the years of child rearing, there have been many learning curves. God has created each of us distinctly and uniquely. No DNA is the same.

The different personalities require varying ways to communicate effectively. We have found the DiSC[1]wellness model a good framework to better understand ourselves and others. The DiSC system should be used in a positive way to encourage a person to be their best, not to label someone.

---

[1] DiSC is a behavioral assessment testing system that allows one to gain insight into the interaction style, personality traits and behavioral tendencies of individuals.

I studied the DiSC model of human behavior early on as a young entrepreneur and shared with my family. We have used this model in all areas of life to better communicate. The DiSC model types include 4 personality traits.

D – Dominant – outgoing and task-oriented. They tend to say what they think and express their opinions as facts. They talk about achievements, plans, and goals.

I – Influence – Outgoing and people-oriented. People interest them, and they tend to watch others. They are animated when they talk; they tell people stories and like to talk about themselves. They are the life of the party.

S- Steady – Reserved and people oriented. Easy going, outwardly calm. They listen carefully and seem engaged. They rarely talk about themselves; family is very important to them.

C- Compliant – Careful, detailed, task-oriented. Reserved and quiet. They usually prefer written communication. Big on details. They study the specifics. Focus on data, facts, and figures, not feelings and opinions.

For the best engagement and understanding, I've found these strategies to work best in communicating with the DiSC personality types.

D – you must provide direct answers and act quickly. Try not to repeat yourself. Focus on bottom line issues and results.

I – maintain a positive atmosphere. Allow them to express themselves. Be more expressive and enthusiastic. Paint the picture. Don't talk too long or give too much information at once; they bore easily. Tell stories, give illustrations. Give recognition to them. Focus on the people aspect.

S – communicate in a logical way and don't rush the conversation. Provide time for them to reflect, provide support, and ask their opinions; listen intently. They need to be heard and understood.

C – be thorough, include all information; discover the key issues and focus on them. Listen carefully, utilizing supporting materials.

This system has allowed us to build trust, resolve problems, provide clarity, increase engagement, improve productivity, promote team spirit and a strong family bond.

Most people possess two of the four traits prominently. For instance, DI or SC; the combination makes up who you most resemble. Once you find out who that person is by conversing and spending time together, you will communicate more effectively easier.

Our children possess three different traits. Sydnee is Steady, Kennedy is Influencing, and Quincy is Dominant. They were a great training ground to learn with and from.

Develop Problem-solving Skills

Every family has problems. Children learn from their parents how to solve problems. If you walk your children through problem-solving skills, this will take them through life.

Remember that life never seems to go as planned. Don't let the detours in life allow your well-thought-out plans to go awry. We have been firm believers in God's plan. One year, the boys were in elementary and middle school. Kenny took on a new job, coaching at Oklahoma State University. We were living in Dallas, TX, and Sydnee was entering her junior year of HS. It was her final year and she graduated in three years. We didn't want her to have to start her final year of high school in a new city at a new school, so we decided to be flexible and make sacrifices.

Kenny and the boys moved to Stillwater for a year, and Sydnee and I stayed in Texas to get her graduated. We visited back and forth on the weekends. Kenny taught the boys how to cook and become self-sufficient; without Mom around, they did things they would normally not do. They had daily chores: Kennedy ran the sweeper, Q took out trash, and Dad cooked and cleaned the kitchen in their small apartment. It was not easy being separated for a year, but we did what had to be done at the time to make the family work. After Sydnee graduated, she took her official senior year and lived in the beautiful city of Napoli, Italy, sitting on the bay of Naples with a student exchange program. I then moved to Stillwater with Kenny and the boys.

We know that life sometimes takes us in a totally different direction, but we must trust God and trust the process. We have always believed that life will work itself out as long as God is our guiding light. Yes, the detours, the roadblocks can be frustrating. We have chosen to believe this season will not last forever.

Accountability

Kenny: Hold family accountable for behavior and attitude. Set family standards. Inspect what you expect. Make sure the playing field is fair. Don't expect to receive and not give. Have each other's back. Be there through the tough times. Love unconditionally.

You should show up in all ways for the people who mean the most to you. I wanted to show my kids how much I loved my wife and how much I supported and respected my wife. If children see that model, they are more inclined to model the behavior. Marriage is a partnership; it takes both parties to create the success.

Part of accountability is learning from your mistakes. Admit when you are wrong and desire to get better. We are all flawed. Flawed individuals create flawed families; therefore, perfection is nonexistent. We do the best we can with what we have to work with, believing today is an opportunity to be better than we were the day before.

Sabrina: Discipline is also a crucial aspect of accountability. Creating a structure you hold your family—and yourself—to. Create structured standards for your household. When boundaries are set and rules are applied, then your family code of conduct is established. We have always put a high priority on education. We would always tell the kids, *work first, play later.* We instilled that hard work is rewarded. My mother always told us to work for great grades. C's were average so don't bring them home. Strive to do your very best. I don't think our children brought many B's home. I literally don't think 2 of our 3 brought a B home until they went to high school, and it was a rarity. We also taught discipline in one area shows up how you live in other areas of life.

I've earned 16 pink Cadillacs in my direct selling career. Every 2-3 years, I take delivery of a brand-new car. Driving the trophy on wheels gets much attention. Little kids wave me down in the neighborhood, people stop me and take pictures of the coveted pink ride, truckers honk at me on the highway and give me a thumbs up, police, at times, forgive my speed. It's been a wonderful thing to drive the dream. Much hard work, commitment, and determination is taken to drive the pink car, the highest standard of excellence in my business. What's better than me driving free is leading others to do the same. I am excited to teach those who want success, how to find it.

One of my team members, who has been building her business for 25 plus years was the first team member I coached to a pink Cadillac. She came from the banking industry and was a calculated thinker; she understood the business was not magical, but mathematical. I told her if she wanted to earn the use of a pink Cadillac she needed numbers, the numbers of people to grow in her organization. We put a strategy together. She was a great student, hungry, and was willing to learn. She was always the first one at our weekly sales meeting, sitting up front, with pen and paper in hand, taking pages and pages of notes. A true example of when the student is ready the teacher will appear. She asked questions for better clarity, and wanted a strategy of success to implement, and didn't mind having daily check-ins. It was important as her mentor to have a trusted accountability system.

This was not a one-way street. I also needed to understand what made this leader tick. I took time to learn how to work with different personality traits, how to bring the best out of my leader. As I coached her to success, I came to know her better. I knew she wanted details in the plan. She was the kind of leader who didn't need the hype. She wanted useful tactics to become a better salesperson, varying ways to attract people to our product and business opportunity. It was a joy to watch her stack small victories daily that added up to her monthly/quarterly/annual success. Her confidence grew over the years; she has created great success, enjoying the livelihood of an independent, successful entrepreneur. It is a leader's dream to duplicate success.

I met this leader on a ski trip in Steamboat, Colorado. I shared the business opportunity with her, and she said yes. Imagine if I never shared the business with her? You never know whose dream is tied to yours.

There is something about high level success that attracts success to you. I always share with my business associates, family, and friends that success begets success.

Success can change the dynamics of your income, lifestyle, and independence. As a mentor, you sometimes face resistance; sometimes the game plan changes, many times the desired results are not met, and there is disappointment that must be worked through. It's all part of the winning process.

I remember being on track to hit goals and then missing them in my business several times. I was sad, mad, and wanted to give up. As I now look back, I realize those experiences have helped me become a better leader.

My definition for the acronym M.A.D is now: MOTIVATED AND DETERMINED!

You must take risks in working with those you lead to become better, stretching them in every way. I stretch the people I work with, encouraging them to get to a bigger, broader, stronger place. Our brains, our bodies, are like rubber bands; expandable, once stretched, we never go back to our original form.

As a leader, the people you coach and desire to be coached must be held accountable for success.

You must ask the hard questions and require the work to be done. Some are willing to be held accountable; others are not. As a mentor, I'm grateful to have had those who held me accountable, kept me focused, helped me work to get to the next level, and create the success I deserved. Success is within reach for all, but you must do what it takes to get it.

Put God First

Sabrina: I am grateful for the foundation laid by my maternal and paternal grandparents, who dragged me to church as a young girl. It was never about whether we wanted to go to church; it was about when were we going and how long we were staying. Thank God for praying grandparents who wanted the future generation to be faith filled and God-centered.

Of course, we wanted the same for our children. Taking our family to church to give honor to God and profess our faith was important to us as we built our family. Our kids knew we were going to church on Sunday morning.

The scripture Psalm 122:1: *I was glad when they said unto me, "Let us go to the house of the LORD,"* reminds us of the importance to worship at church, but we believe that the church is just a building; the people make up the church.

If we weren't traveling to wrestling tournaments or traveling for business, on Sunday AM, our family knew we were going to church. Our children basically grew up in a mega church – the Potter's House in Dallas, Texas pastored by Bishop TD Jakes. This was a huge church with a membership of 30,000. Big church, small town feel. This church fed our souls. Bishop Jakes had a strong, bellowing voice that captured the entire family's attention. We kept the children with us to worship instead of sending them to children's church downstairs. We liked staying together. Church was long too! 11 am 1:30 pm most Sundays.

The kids learned to be still, pay attention, and most importantly get a better understanding of Jesus Christ and strengthen their personal relationships. Their reward most Sundays for being good in church turned into a family tradition which was stopping by the big gas station on the way home for hotdogs and chips.

We learned early on *the family that prays together stays together*. We had to pray our way through many peaks and valleys. The Bible has been our compass for life. Every twist and turn in life, if we didn't turn to God in prayer, we would not be here.

The Power of Love

Kenny: FAMILY is the power of love. Nobody loves you like family. Nobody gives unconditionally like family. Everything that is formulated early on starts with family love and care. The more you get love, the more love you give. I remember playing sandlot football. I was the youngest playing with the big kids. In order to play, I had to be courageous and tough. As the youngest and smallest, I was the one always looking up. I also looked up to the examples of love in my family, love of each other, love of life, love of sport, competition and winning.

Strong family structure is important to adopt values and learn lifelong lessons that you carry into adulthood. My parents divorced when I was in high school, however, I was blessed to capture examples of love and leadership while growing up.

In my life, I also saw examples of family life that wasn't positive, including drugs, addiction, abuse, and divorce. Observing that behavior helped me learn and understand this wasn't a model I wanted for my family, and I had to work hard not to succumb to becoming a statistic to what was prevalent in my community, destroying the fabric of the Black family. One must be aware and live with intention not to fall into the trap of family dysfunction.

Family support has been key to our success. When we talk about family, it goes beyond immediate family. We develop a family atmosphere when we work closely with the people we coach or mentor. In my world, in order to maximize your effectiveness with your athletes, it's crucial that you develop trust.

One of my greatest examples of building that trust happened while coaching Coleman Scott to an Olympic bronze medal at the 2012 Olympic Games. When I first accepted the job as head coach of the Regional Training Center program at Oklahoma State University, Coleman was ranked 3rd in the USA. Coleman had never beaten the No. 1 ranked man in 3 matches, and the number 2 ranked wrestler, he hadn't beat in two years. It was 2010 and the 2012 Olympic Games were two years away, so we had a lot of work to do in a short period of time.

One of the first things I wanted to do was get to know Coleman and let him get to know me, my wife, and kids so I invited him to our house for dinner. We spent the next two hours getting to know each other, talking about our families and his plans to one day have a family of his own. We both understood that in order to reach our goals of making that 2012 Olympic team, we were going to need to trust one another and believe in the plan I laid out for him. My system was a little different from the system he had been accustomed to, so that first year, we made progress but not at the level he would need in order to beat the best guys in the world. That first year was crucial because it gave us a foundation of trust that allowed me to train Coleman harder than he had ever been trained before! There were some very uncomfortable moments when the intensity of our training sessions was high. He would ask if they were necessary. I would always reply, "Very."

The fact that we had developed such a close family like relationship gave us the ability to reach higher heights. The next year, he jumped levels and beat the No. 2, then the No. 1 wrestler in the US who he had not beaten ever, which afforded him the chance to make the USA 2016 Olympic team in RIO and win a bronze medal.

Family and friends provide comfort in good times and bad. Studies have shown that having supportive relationships is a strong protective factor against mental illness and helps to increase our mental well-being.

Notes/Reflections

FIRE

Sabrina: Fire is the energy and passion in our lives, our families, our businesses, and our faith. It is the burning motivation that keeps you moving, working, and thinking of the next thing. Fire also spreads. What we mean by that is when we strive daily to be on fire, those around us seem to *catch it*. One of my greatest mentors, Sean Key, based out of a Dallas, Texas, said, "Sabrina, if you are surrounding yourself with folks not on fire, you better set yourself on fire!" He was great at giving me a swift kick in the butt when I needed it. I set myself on fire by hitting goals, resetting the goal, and pushing myself out of my comfort zone. The new goals create excitement and passion.

There have been times in life, in love, marriage, business, and pleasure when everything was sizzling hot. Other times, life has been lukewarm, and let's be honest: At times, life can be downright cold. Brrrrrrr. The chilly times, I didn't like. I was disinterested, uninvolved, not engaged, simply going through the motions, doing my best to make it through the day. When the temperature is chilly, you tend to doubt yourself and others around you; you may have a bad attitude. You may not be feeling like yourself, and depression can sink in. It is important to recognize your state of being and work to flip the switch. Turn things around.

BE A FIRE STARTER!

Sabrina: When you are on fire, everything you touch seems to turn to gold; all the lights are green, nothing can stop you, you are all the way up. Passion adds fuel to the fire!

You cannot stroll to the goal. You must work with a sense of urgency. When you are full of fire, it's not business as usual.

Think to when you have had those winning seasons. They first started with winning hours, which then moved into winning days. Your enthusiasm for life ignites the world. Your passion creates synergy and energy. You work on walking into a room, making sure your positive presence is felt. You decide to easily make friends, and believe people want to know you; they want to hear what you have to say. Your passion permeates and fills up the spaces you occupy.

Sometimes you have to move on that burning flicker inside of your soul, even when nobody else understands what it is. I had that burning desire in 2012 to build my business internationally, to build a global market. It was a tall endeavor. All expenses were on me: travel, food, translator, housing, grit, and determination. My first market to pursue was Brazil, many miles away, and an eight-hour plane ride. Building from scratch, working 15-hour days, leaving my family, and the investment of time, money, and energy were a big commitment, and the payoff was little. I learned a lot, but the dividends did not pay quickly on my investment.

The flicker of the flame was dimmed but still there. I wasn't ready to give up on my global dreams. I wanted to give another global market a chance. A couple of years later, I took the lessons and took my talents to Colombia, South America. I love the people, the music, the food, and the flowers. I fell in love with Medellin, the City of Eternal Spring, 75 degrees 365 days a year. The time zone was the same, the travel was relatively easy – a 4-hour plane ride from Fort Lauderdale. I better understood the peso currency. I had a translator, a wonderful woman, Sonia Nango-Henesy who would accompany me there. My husband blessed the deal, and the kids were supportive of my dreams. I made many trips, at one point, going every 90 days for 2 years, building and building some more.

Speaking very little Spanish other than the basics, and huge thanks to my translation team, I now have hundreds of team members in Colombia with great leaders. So many people told me it wasn't safe, that I needed to build bigger first in the US, that it wasn't worth my time. I'm so glad I followed my flame.

Because my fire was burning bright, now the fire burns bright for many others.

The average monthly income for a college educated woman in Colombia is equivalent to $750. Now those women have quadrupled that salary with their businesses, work from home, and spend quality time with their families.

One of those women I mentored is a former bank executive, married to a doctor, whose dream was to be able to have a home-based business. Another leader is an entrepreneur; they had a small restaurant selling empanadas, a delightful crispy pastry that is filled with chicken or beef, sometimes veggies and cheese. Her husband also owned a taxi, and they both left those businesses and devoted their lives to building their own businesses. Their highest combined income in one month exceeded any previous income they had ever earned. That income was higher pay than some of the wealthiest government officials, doctors, and lawyers in the country. This is another example of you never know whose dream is tied to yours. Be a fire starter today!

DESIRE

It's important to have a strong feeling of desire, wanting something or wishing for something to happen. Your desire moves you toward your goals. Desire keeps you excited and willing to proceed with your dreams. Desire is fueled by your why. You must make sure there is a clear desire for what you want to accomplish. If you don't, you will easily quit when the going gets tough. Desire makes you grit your teeth and work it out. When desire is strong, determination is stronger. Desire also gives you inspiration and energy.

Dreams don't become reality if the desire is not strong. Desire is connected to your purpose. Desire is the flame that continues to flicker inside of you. Desire is the thing that makes you uncomfortable. Desire is your guiding light and is the foundation that you build from.

Desire allows you to live life out loud, unapologetically. Strive to work and walk within a particular calling upon your life. When your desire is high, life is purposeful, fulfilling, and exhilarating. When life is not lived with desire, you are unfulfilled. There is a void, and you feel empty, as if you should be doing more.

You must create and increase your desire. Don't give yourself an out. Make a deal with yourself, honor your word to yourself, make the desire public, and state the desire to those you respect. Allow them to hold you accountable; constantly remind yourself why you want what you want. Allow your dreams to be the compass for your desires.

Visualize your rewards for keeping your desire high and match your work ethic to your desire. Surround yourself with like-minded people. They will not let your desire or deserve level dwindle. The people around you should stretch you. You should be inspired by what others are doing around you. It's hard to not be desirous when everybody else in your circle is.

INTENTION

Focus your intention. Your energy flows where your intention goes. When creating fire, your focus is keen. Your fire burns brightly when focus is high. Your intention should deeply resonate with you. It should make you jump out of bed each morning and make it difficult for you to go to bed at night. A hard focus allows you to leave your fears behind. When you are on fire, your fear dissipates. You are so focused on the task at hand, you move around fear. You set daily goals with the intention of giving it your best. You don't major in the minors; you control what you can control. The road to success comes with great adversity, however, when you are focused, you make up your mind that you will overcome whatever life throws at you with calm and conviction.

I like to use the Persian adage, "This too shall pass" when I'm thrown off my center. Yes, life comes upon choppy waters. However, we know the storms don't last forever. Get back in the boat and oar to shore. Do not let life's distractions keep you from accomplishing greatness.

CREATIVITY

Through creativity, there are many paths that help you find the courage to be better every day. Creative thinkers find ways to get better, do things differently, and improve constantly. They demonstrate persistence in using their imagination to not be brought down by their obstacles. You must think differently to stand out.

When the goal is big, you think a different thought. You become more creative with your unique ideas and birth dreams. Opportunities come to creative people because they look for them. When you are creative, you learn to make things exciting and enjoyable. You find flexibility in applying knowledge, think outside the box, and do things in a way never done before. You bring a fresh perspective to the idea and it's easier to engage others. People want new, fresh, exciting thoughts and ideas.

Excitement brings people together. Include them in your vision. When you speak, speak with enthusiasm. The energy you bring to the project is what you will get in return. Don't worry about everybody being on board with your idea, your plan, or project. Find the few who will bring the fire. Define a theme, have a song, and create a visually appealing campaign. Energize the group to get the buy in. If you are boring as a presenter, it's hard to sell the sizzle. People buy what you sell. Make sure it's hot!

WORK WITH PEOPLE YOU LIKE

It's important to work with people you like. It's easier to create fire with people you enjoy, people who are re-latable, people who you vibe with. Life is too hard to do life with people that don't value your vision. When you are self-employed, it's easier said than done. You often don't get to choose, so you make the best of the situation. My motto has always been *it's my job to get along with people, not their job to get along with me.*

GIVE OF YOURSELF

"Ask not what your country can do for you, but what you can do for your country." John F. Kennedy challenged every American to contribute in some way to the public good.

There is always somebody who can benefit from your gifts. Give your gifts always.

Always seek to make a difference. The masthead on our family's newspaper which was started by my grandfather 100 years ago states, "We make America better when we aide our people." It's a simple reminder to help others in any way possible. Many times, we are at our best when we are giving of ourselves.

BUILD ON SMALL VICTORIES

Instead of focusing on all that needs to be done, all that hasn't been done, take inventory of what's already been done and what you are doing. Remember what Desmond Tutu once said: "There is only one way to eat an elephant: a bite at a time."

FEED AND SATISFY YOUR SOUL

Do things that make you feel alive. Be with people who lift you, not drain you. Go after a life that feels good – you deserve it! Take time to declutter, breathe, let go emotionally and physically to anything that no longer holds value to you. Spend time with nature; it helps you to destress and relax.

It's important to know yourself, so you can know when your gas tank is running low. You have to refuel.

Here are some other ways to refuel:

- Travel
- Seeing loved ones
- Special dinner outing
- Going to church
- Meditation
- Massages
- Spending time with friends and family
- Taking a break
- Going on vacation
- Find your inspiration
- Grow in the environment

Music can also help set you on fire. Some of my favorite fire songs include:

1. "Fire," by Earth, Wind, and Fire
2. "Ain't no Stopping Us Now," by McFadden and Whitehead
3. "You Can't Touch This," by MC Hammer
4. "Boom Boom Pow" by Black Eyed Peas

5. "Blow the Whistle" by Too Short...and anything by Bruno Mars.

These are my go-to songs that alter my fire mood! Find music that ignites your soul and puts a bounce in your step.

STRETCH YOURSELF

You must have goals that motivate you. When I don't have a goal, I am less inclined to have fire. Does fire fuel your dreams or do dreams fuel your fire? For me, my dreams fuel the fire. Over the years, it's been my marriage, my children, my family, and/or my career that motivated me to want to be better. Knowing the goal is not the end. It is a means to the end. When you are a go-getter, it's never about the destination, always the journey.

I am married to a man who stays on fire. He is a 3x Olympian, now a coach, full of fire. When he comes from work, he is still fired up while sometimes, I'm winding down. However, if he comes into the house full of energy, excited about life, and pumped up, I can't help but mirror his energy. One person can shift the energy of the household.

When there is no fire, the mood is somber, laid back, quiet, and unenthusiastic.

The power of one can make the difference. Take control of your environment.

We vacationed in beautiful St. Croix. We wanted a quick getaway where no passports were needed since our college-aged sons had misplaced theirs. COVID cases were rising, and we just wanted to steal away some sun and fun with family before the summer ended.

It was a fabulous vacay. We were all on fire!

We hadn't had a vacation because of the pandemic in almost two years. Breathing in the ocean air, getting plenty of Vitamin D, spending a few days in paradise with the Caribbean Sea sparked my fire.

Life had become a bit stale. The 24-hour news cycle had become my best friend, and I was overwhelmed with the daily daunting news of COVID 19, and then the Delta variant. A few days of sea, sand, and self-care along with not carrying the weight of the world while watching the 2020 Olympic Games from our seaside villa gave me newfound fire!

Watching the Olympics with an Olympian is a rich experience. You get to relive his 3 trips to the Olympic

Games, Seoul, Korean '88, Barcelona, Spain in '92, and Atlanta, Georgia in '96. You hear the backstories. It's quite inspiring.

USA wrestling was highly successful this cycle. Our household was ecstatic, and the neighbors could hear our screams for the USA team. Tokyo 2020 was postponed to the summer of 2021, because of the pandemic. Even then, these games, granted limited access to those who wanted to attend, to watch. This was touted to be one of the greatest games ever for USA wrestling, bringing 9 medals home, just barely losing the team title to Russia.

Heavyweight Gable Stevenson made his first Olympic wrestling team at twenty- one years old while still in college at Minnesota. He broke all belief barriers, bringing home the GOLD! He did his signature backflip after his Gold medal match. To see a guy of his size throw himself in the air was almost as exciting as the winning match itself.

Gable was full of fire, beating his opponent in a last-second move to grab the win! That thrilling victory will go down in history.

His fire, his passion to win, giving it all he had until the end gave my entire family fire that morning that carried us throughout the day. We were ENERGIZED the rest of the vacay by his victory. Did you know that the probability of winning a Gold medal is 0.000003%? Yes, approximately 1 in 3.5 million. Even though you are fully absorbed, super passionate about your life's sport, practice day and night for 4 years, 8 years, most athletes will never win an Olympic Gold medal. Our family is forever proud of our very own OLYMPIAN KENNY MONDAY.

ENERGY FROM THE FLAMES

Sabrina: Energy is one of my best attributes. I am intentional about creating it, keeping it, and spreading it to others. I work at transferring the contagious spirit of hope, love, light, and laughter to all I encounter. I do believe my fire that I work to light from within has created much of my success in various areas of my life. I have been purposeful in keeping my vibrations high; your vibration is your mental and emotional state of being. When it's high, you feel more confident and in touch with yourself.

It started early, when I was crowned 7th grade homecoming queen, to radiate life with a megawatt smile, going on to become Carver Middle School homecoming queen, continuing to spread positivity at my high school, Booker T. Washington, and becoming the football homecoming Queen, both in Tulsa, Oklahoma, where I was born and raised. I then took my FLAME to college, where I was named Miss Freshman and then ultimately crowned College Queen, Miss Tennessee State University in Nashville, where I was invited back to be the Grand Marshall at our homecoming fall 2021.

People are attracted to Passion, Purpose and Power. People want to be surrounded by fire in all stages of life. You give it, you get it. If you are negative, whining, complaining, and pessimistic, nobody is inspired by you. Decide to change; work on yourself. Your life is a never-ending project to get better.

WINNING REQUIRES ENTHUSIASM!

Kenny: My fire and passion come from my goals. My fire comes from me wanting to be the best. Watching champions, studying how champions carry themselves, motivated me to work hard and dream big. I love competing, learning, and trying new things. My fire was lit when learning how to perform and compete. Also, to learn a new skill set, practice it, and see it work was satisfying!

I had a knack for learning a new technique and implementing my style. I hear people say I was one of the most exciting wrestlers in the history of the sport. I was always trying new skills and becoming creative with different moves. I was always intrigued by the technical side of wrestling. I liked to explore, I wanted to entertain, I wanted people to come to see me compete. I remember when I was in college going for the pin record. I wanted to have the most pins by a wrestler at Oklahoma State University in Stillwater, OK. The sports director told me I had 10 more pins to break an all-time record.

The school decided to build a promotion around the countdown to the record. People were excited! They couldn't wait to come to the matches. I had 25 matches left to get the 10 pins in for the year. The year was exciting and filled with anticipation.

I got down to my final 2 pins. There was one match on a Saturday and one on Monday. With the Saturday match, I was trying my best to pin the kid. I had him on his back 5-6 times. He kept getting up, but I beat him 253, but no pin!

The next match was on Monday against Illinois. They built the contest: "Don't miss Monday on Monday for the record!"

The Gallagher Iba arena was packed! Everybody came to the gym to watch me break the record; we sold the place out! Adrenaline was running high! The crowd was on fire!

I was fired up to get the record on Monday night. I was competing against a good wrestler. The band was there, the cheerleaders were there, and all kinds of media showed up! There was a lot of pressure for me to make it happen.

The 1st period of a three-period match, I didn't do it! The 2nd period, I didn't do it. It got down to the 3rd period with 45 seconds left. I got it done in the 3rd period with 45 seconds left. YES, I got it done!

The fire fueled me. I secured my 51st pin for the record. History was made! The Pin record for Oklahoma State University was established! The record was held from 1984 to 2014 -- 30 years!

SHARING THAT ENTHUSIASM

Much of my fire and enthusiasm for the sport of wrestling came from me being the underdog. When I first started competing, wrestling was dominated by mostly white athletes; we had a predominately African American team, we were new to the sport, not very skilled, and not funded. Our opponents seemed to have a new uniform for every match while we wore the same outfit all year.

My motivation was to change the landscape, create a movement of young, black successful wrestlers making a difference in the sport. I wanted to help kids be competitive and fall in love with the sport. I wanted our team to be relevant, taken seriously, and compete with the best in the city.

My parents and coaches created exciting opportunities including sleepovers, parties, and camps to make the sport attractive and create staying power. I was a leader in the movement at a young age. I knew winning was important and bringing back trophies to the YMCA intrigued others and made them more interested in what we were doing.

Trophies made a difference. A big part of wrestling are the trophies that are awarded. The trophy life reward system created fire. There are lots of individual trophies given out. Unlike other sports, where team trophies are presented, wrestling is an individual sport with several different weight classes, so you go for the individual and the team award.

Trophy life includes plaques, medals, and trophies. At the beginning of the tournament, they would be all lined up on the display table. You thought about the awards throughout the tourney. My house was filled with all kinds of trophies throughout the years. The same thing that motivated me motivated my sons. They started wrestling at 5 and 6 and started filling the house up with trophies as well.

Winning is contagious.

Momentum builds on itself; people wanted to be part of the success we created.

We had guys who had never wrestled come out for the team.

Wrestling changes kids' lives. Many find the sport when they are too little to play football or basketball. They find a spot for themselves in wrestling. Wrestling gives discipline, purpose, individual and team success. Those who wrestled also became better in other sports.

I had a teammate in high school -- Booger Paul Parker. He was huge, approximately 6' 3, 265 lbs. He was a gentle giant, afraid of his own shadow. He started wrestling, his confidence grew, and he started dressing better, developed charisma, even started talking to the girls. He became a 2x State Champion and went on to become a recipient of a full ride football scholarship at Oklahoma University in Norman, OK, where he was a 4-year starter under legendary coach Barry Switzer.

Wrestling practices are tough. It has always been important for me to go in with high energy. When energy is high, practices are exciting. Every environment is better when positive vibes are flowing. The passion creates magic, a great learning environment. People respond to high vibrations.

For me as a competitor, passion helps you to enjoy the sport. You must be serious but create a fun, competitive environment. It's not personal, it's competition. Sometimes coaches forget about giving good energy and the sport is not fun. Look for positivity when teaching, sharing, coaching, and creating an uplifting experience. For people to come in and not enjoy what you do, it is evident you need to do something different.

I've seen coaches critically put athletes down coaching

out of fear and punishment. It doesn't work. For instance, "If you don't do this right, you will run 10 extra sprints." I've left situations that were not positive when I didn't like going to practice with coaches that were miserable.

It's important to help teammates through adversity. Team building exercises make the difference. There is no I in Team. Teamwork makes the dream work! I especially understood this as my high school wrestling team won 4 straight state championship titles.

FIRE SIGNS

Sabrina is a Leo, born August 7th. Leo traits include warmth and creativity, a little bit vain, really big personality, wants to stand out, interested in luxury. The ruling planet is the sun.

Kenny is a Sagittarius, born November 25th. Sagittarius traits include curious, travelers, idealistic, generous, great sense of humor, extrovert, optimistic, enthusiasm has no boundaries.

Leo and Sagittarius are FIRE SIGNS. We get the FIRE honestly. We work hard not to crash and burn. It takes work.

Here's another quick pneumonic to ignite your fire:

F: Fuel the FIRE

Ignite the flame. Find purpose in your living.

I: Insight

Insight requires you to delve deep into your why, the purpose for what you do. Your why should make you cry. You will not easily give up your passionate goals if your why is big and meaningful.

R: Redefine

Sometimes your goals get lost in the busyness of life. You will need to redefine and update them to keep them fresh on your mind.

E: Expect

Expect greatness! Have an attitude of expectancy. Look at the glass half full.

Believe in yourself and what you are ON FIRE FOR!

Notes/Reflections

Monday Family
Holiday Card
Collection

FORMULA

Kenny: One of the most important lessons I learned was in my first year in wrestling. It shaped and defined my character for the rest of my life and showed me the importance of a repeatable formula for success.

When I was a beginner, I was the smallest kid on my team. I only weighed 43 lbs., soaking wet. The next biggest kid was named Winky. Winky weighed 52 lbs. and was a couple years older. Plus, he had been wrestling for a couple of years, so he had more experience as well. Every day at practice, Winky would get the best of me. It was really bad in the beginning. I couldn't even score a point on him. Everything I tried, he would just counter and use his size and skill to pin me.

I would get so frustrated, but our coach would simply say, "Quitters never win, and winners never quit! Winners win! So just keep coming back, and someday you will be a champion."

So, I did. Every day, I would show up with a good attitude and a smile on my face and try harder and harder. Those words never left me. They became my battle cry. By the end of the wrestling season, I had closed the gap on Winky and started to score points, but I also gained 7 lbs. the next year. He could no longer beat me, and a champion's mindset was born.

I'm incredibly thankful I learned the concept of *winners never quit* early in my life and watched the results play out in real time. From that moment on, it became a part of my formula for success. I use that mentality in every situation that I encountered.

Formulas are a proven tool for creating success. Although there is no single formula that works for everyone, creating personal and professional formulas for yourself can help you achieve your desires. Sabrina has formulas for creating success in her direct sales business. I have formulas that have worked as an athlete and as a coach. And we both have derived formulas to create a winning family.

WINNING NOT WORKING

Sabrina: Our focus has always been on winning not working. When you focus on winning, the work is less cumbersome. You have more energy, and your work is creative and focused. When teaching success formulas to my colleagues, I often summarize it like this: You first need to think of ideas and creativity to form a vision. Then you need a strategy to know how to execute. You need to know who you are partnering with.

Finally, you must be bold. These are the key variables in a winning formula.

Our formula starts with a vision. Mary Kay Ash was a visionary leader. She wanted to create a company by a woman for women. She saw that her company would change women's lives worldwide. She believed when you give a woman a business that builds confidence, she can conquer the world.

One day, I got a note from one of my consultants on my team. She is an attorney in Raleigh, Durham with a private practice, working her part-time MK business and recently widowed. She wrote, "Sabrina, I really appreciate you; you may not realize it, but you and the Mary Kay philosophy have helped me to take a personal inventory and work wonders in my life."

Sixty years after the inception of MK, lives are being blessed by the thousands.

And that success comes from a winning formula. The MK formula for success is still one of the most admired and studied around the world.

Kenny: When I was a little kid, I was intrigued when I saw this national magazine that featured a young Mongolian wrestler on the cover in his native dress. As a kid, I didn't look much past my neighborhood, let alone another country. I didn't realize they wrestled outside the US. That visual sparked a thought inside of me. I thought, *one day, it would be cool to go to Mongolia and wrestle.*

I captured the vision from a magazine what wrestling was and could be. It created a vision of wrestling all over the world. It took me from my neighborhood to the city, other states, throughout the country, and all over the world. If they were competing worldwide, I wanted to be the best in the world. Not only did I get to compete in Mongolia in 1987, but I won the World Cup. Now I teach the importance of envisioning yourself on a world stage competing in wrestling.

In order to create a vision for your formula, you must first learn about your goals. Research the subject matter. Get to know your area of interest so you can create a truly effective formula.

Next, make it real by writing it down and sharing your goals with other people. Talk about it. Flush out your thoughts and concerns. In talking through the ideas, you will better understand what you want the project to be.

Creativity is at the core of any vision. To encourage your own creativity, start by uncluttering. Clear your mind. Clear your work area to make a space that allows your creative juices to flow. Talk to like-minded people to get ideas you may not have thought of yourself. Get inspired by music, others, and deadlines. Find your formula for creativity and use it.

You must see the world to change the world. A clear vision of what you want to accomplish is crucial. It is the map to your future success. Your thoughts must manifest a greater desire from within. The discipline of creating a vision for yourself is a formula for success.

BETWEEN VISION AND
SUCCESS IS STRATEGY

A well-thought-out strategy is a critical part of a formula for success. Start by defining your targets. What are your goals? If it's a business venture, what is your market audience? Know who you are looking for and why. Have a keen eye, a focused mindset.

Focus on systematic growth. Give yourself a timetable to make things happen; put systems in place to grow your organization. Consistent systems that create growth will give you necessary traceable, trackable results.

Make fact-based decisions. It is easy to get caught up in emotions while creating a formula. You must not do what feels good; you have to do what makes sense. Follow the facts.

Think long-term and conquer your goals. In your formula for success, we always teach to work with the end in mind. You can think about the most effective strategy to get from a starting point to that end goal.

BUILD A TEAM

Kenny: Another great concept I was taught during those early years was the value of teamwork and teammates. Being the youngest on the team had its advantages and disadvantages. One of the main advantages was that everyone wanted to help me get better. Our coach was intentional on stressing the value of being a great teammate and that was the glue that held the team together. Those two fundamental principles— teamwork and teammates—are the backbone of success.

I started to understand how to get better, the fundamentals of how to utilize your resources, and how to apply what you've learned in order to achieve your goals. It was crystal clear to me. I had to be very intentional and very observant.

First and foremost, you need to know yourself and what motivates you. What's the best way for you to learn, whether it is visual or hands on. Everyone is different. I am very visual. I studied the best kids on the team. I watched the way they carried themselves and how they responded to the coaches and teammates. I always made a point when we went to compete at wrestling tournaments to watch the best kids, the champions of the tournament. I paid close attention to everything they did, from how they warmed up to how they competed to how they handled their wins as well as their losses. I even watched the way they interacted with the referees, which turned out to be a huge part of my success.

I wanted to win at everything I did and was always very competitive. I think it's very important to have great coaches and mentors early in life. If you learn good fundamentals in the beginning, you don't need to be taught those lessons later. I really thrived in being a part of a team and working together for a common goal.

The formula for a winning team starts with having like-minded people, all on the same page, working for the universal goal. If you don't agree on what winning looks like, you're unlikely to win.

You also need partners to complement your own ideas. Be inclusive. Different backgrounds mean different ways of looking at the world. That leads to more creativity, more comprehensive strategies, and a stronger team. It also allows you to challenge each other. Your team should make you think a different thought. It can't be comfortable. Know your way is not the only way and be open to other ideas.

Teammates should help each other, but they should also be competitive. You must strive to outwork others. The race always makes you run harder. Don't back down from the competition. Iron sharpens iron.

Sabrina: Remember, you cannot be all things to all people. Everybody must work in their strengths. You don't have to be good at everything. Work in your strengths and hire or partner for what you need. Exercise your muscle in areas that create growth and excellence and let others focus on the rest.

You'll also need to develop thick skin. Stop getting your feelings hurt easily.

Toughen up! Ask for what you need. A closed mouth does not get fed! My daddy used to say that all the time. I'm not pushy; I'm pleasantly persistent. You must ASK to GET!

A successful team's winning formula is giving back. A partnership goes both ways.

Make people feel important. In working with people, name recognition is important. People love hearing the sound of their name. Learn people's songs and learn how to sing it. This will allow you to inspire the fire.

Finally, choose God as your power partner. Appreciate the gift of life you have been given and remember faith and fear cannot coexist. Choose one, and we hope you choose faith.

BE BOLD

When your dream is big enough, the facts don't matter. A truly successful formula is boldness; you have to put bold into action. Be in it to win it. Own your power. Be a *goal digger*. Stay out of your head. It's like a bad neighborhood. You should never go there alone.

Entrepreneurship is not for the faint of heart. You will be rejected, but rejection is not personal. When they say *no*, I say *next*. Take the rejection and turn *no* into ***it's on***!

Find your reason, and don't detour from your dream. Working will win where wishing won't. You must create the life you deserve to have. Use these tools that we have discussed to win. Winning is your birthright. A life of options and opportunities awaits you. When you embrace boldness, you will get noticed. Make a name for yourself!

Take this mantra and run with it: "We don't just do;

we outdo." The formula for leadership is simple: Be the leader. LEAD YOUR SHIP.

Be who you say you are. Be kind and never cocky. Don't sweat the small stuff.

When you really think about it, it's all small. Authenticity, kindness, and perspective will draw the right people to you.

FAMILY FORMULA

Sabrina: Our family's formula for success basically includes mindset strategies, an understanding that has helped our family over the years that can be adopted and adapted for your particular family situation. We believe our family's formulas can also be useful for other families.

Success is not always convenient. To achieve it, I found you must get rid of the mommy-guilts. When managing a busy family's lifestyle, it is challenging to be several places at once or be all things to all people. I have told my children for years, as we managed the many extra-curricular activities, ran a home-based business, and supported my husband in his many endeavors, that I will miss some things, but I will make more than I miss. My kids understood, early on, how important they were to us as parents, however, life is full of compromise and balance.

Kenny: One of the very first areas of concentration that I focus on when developing kids is their confidence, their belief system. I believe it's crucial to create an environment where kids can thrive and feel that they are important to the team's success, even if they are not one of the best on the team. I want them to understand the power of belief! I teach them that no one should ever believe in them more than they believe in themselves. Mental development is so much more important than physical development at an early age. If kids or any athletes have a healthy and solid view of themselves, then it makes them easier to coach. Sometimes you need to build them up before they can start to learn and enjoy the process.

Kids come in at all levels of belief, so I take them at whatever level they're at and start the building process. Once I get the mental aspect figured out and healthy, then we start working on the physical aspect. I build the head and the body follows. That was the blueprint of my success early, and I just mastered it through the years. Some kids come to me with a lot of fear. They are scared of losing, scared of losing parents' approval, scared of being embarrassed, or scared of what their friends will say if they fail. Part of that formula of success is teaching my athletes how to manage fear or to allow fear to work for you and not against you.

FORMULAS ARE VARIABLE

Formulas change, based on projects and players. You must be free to create the right strategy for success and work with the right people. Be ready to adjust your formula as necessary. Many times, the reason we stray from a formula for success is that we are not patient with the process. We want the finished product so badly and are not patient with ourselves or the formula itself. Be patient. Once you find a formula, stick to it. Measure your results and execute according to your plan. If you see room for improvement, add those improvements to your formula and use it again.

As I travel internationally, I teach the same foundational principles in business as in the States. You must have hustle, grace, grit, and stamina, as well as a repeatable formula for success. There is a branding concept called Step and Repeat. Basically, it is a message, usually from a company, that is repetitive and visual. It makes the consumer remember and recall the brand, the messaging, more easily. Our formulas are that way. To be effective, a formula must be engrained in your brain. Consistency and repetition of winning habits create a life well lived.

If you don't have proven formulas that work for you and are implemented often, you are always trying a new way, another way, or failed ways that don't bring you your desired success. In life, you must find a formula, winning systems, that work for you and those you care most about. Nothing comes to sleepers but a dream. Now, wake up! Go to work and turn your dreams into a reality.

Notes/Reflections

FORGIVENESS

In life, we experience love, grace, acceptance, rejection, and death and then there is forgiveness, which is absolutely necessary to move forward. We must all learn to forgive. Forgiveness can be difficult, sometimes never achieved, however, striving toward it is important. Forgiveness helps the forgiver more than the person you are forgiving. It frees you up. A lack of forgiveness allows you to harbor ill feelings and keeps you stuck.

We are all flawed. There are no perfect people. It's important as you go through life to identify those people with ill intent and run. Then there are those who mean well and make mistakes, mistakes that hurt others, sometimes to those we love most.

Sabrina: I grew up with an alcoholic father. He was a sweet, smart man who had an addiction. Unfortunately, alcohol and drug abuse destroy individuals and families. My Dad fought it for years. He caused great chaos in our family, coming home drunk, saying and doing things to my mother that were harmful. He turned into a different person under the influence of alcohol.

As a child, it was difficult to differentiate between the two people he represented. As I got older, I better understood the disease of alcoholism. After many years of turmoil and turbulence, my mom divorced my dad when I was in high school. I was glad. I supported the divorce. I wanted peace in our home. My mother deserved better.

My daddy wanted to do better. The addiction was difficult to overcome, as most addictions are. I always loved my dad but there were times I didn't like him. I remember when he wasn't there. The drinking made him miss important parts of my life, and I missed important parts of his.

Growing up, we lived right across the way from my middle school. I remember, as a kid, being a cheerleader at Carver. It was game day, and my dad hadn't been home in two or three days, and he would show up at the game. That's what happened when he would binge drink. We got used to him being gone. The family didn't really discuss it; we just knew. As we held our pep rally outside, my dad appeared, drunk as a skunk. He was dancing and hollering my name. My friends knew I was embarrassed. Of course, my dad remembered none of it.

When he was sober, he was one of the smartest, kindest men I've ever known.

He went to college at 16. Those who knew him remember him as a walking encyclopedia. He was a true newspaper man, an integral part of our family newspaper; he knew everybody, all the facts, and everybody knew him. Our family newspaper is the oldest minority newspaper in the state of Oklahoma, still owned by my family.

God bless my dad's soul. He passed away July 25, 2014 at 78. He had been sober for many years, I'm happy to say. It took him a long time to get there, with a lot of prayer and discipline. As I look back, I see the good in my dad more so than the bad. Living with addiction is tough. We have it throughout our family, like many families. The hurt, distrust, and uncertainty cause great pain.

For a kid, having two versions of my dad was a lot to process. I was angry at him. I loved him, therefore, I had to forgive him—for me. It took years to forgive him. As I became a young adult and understood his pain and his desire to mask his hurt, I developed a better understanding and was able to take the focus off of me and put it on him. Loving my dad, understanding that it hurt him to hurt his family, coming to know that living a sober life was not easy for him, was a revelation for me on the road to forgiveness. When I forgave my Dad, I felt lighter; I was not as fearful for what might happen to him. My daily prayer was for my dad to get sober. I decided that I would pray for him daily, believing that God would answer my prayers. I did give it to God. When you do, you have the ability to love more, do more, and be more.

Unforgiveness makes you an angry person. If you don't forgive, you will find yourself always going back to a place that upsets you, that agitates you, that keeps you bound. When you practice forgiveness in one area of life, it's easier to forgive in other areas of life. When I forgive, my heart is more open to boundless love, life, and unlimited opportunities. My energy is high, and I am freer to be my best version of myself. When you truly have a forgiving spirit, you also are able to see the best in other people.

Do not live in the pit of an unforgiving heart. You won't forget, but you must get yourself free and forgive.

One of my favorite scriptures on forgiveness is Luke 6:37: "Do not judge others, and you will not be judged. Do not condemn others, or it will all come back against you. Forgive others, and you will be forgiven."

I'm grateful for my mom, the most positive person I have ever known who was not judgmental. She chose to stand tall and not harbor hurtful feelings no matter what. I'm not totally there yet, no lie. She never said a negative word to us about our father. Her thought was, when we are old enough, we will formulate our own opinions. Such a great life lesson, that no matter the pain one presents, do not be judgmental and pray for a forgiving heart.

Forgiveness contributes to your happiness, and happiness is important to your well-being. Forgiveness is an act you do for your peace of mind. That is the real essence of forgiveness—your own tranquility.

TEN STEPS TO FORGIVENESS

Forgiveness is also a process. You can't simply decide to forgive, and the pain and disappointment disappear. You have to work at it to build that power within yourself. Be patient with yourself and others. The following steps are what we follow to reach forgiveness.

Step 1. Leave the past behind you

Sabrina: Life is to be lived. In living, our many experiences shape us. We must learn to accept the good with the bad. Your past is that –- **the past**, and it should stay there.

Work diligently to get better, not bitter. Don't let your past dictate your future. I've found myself stuck in stuff when I'm not willing to push pass the past. Sitting there, mad, as the world goes on, you only hurt yourself when you don't learn from situations and keep moving in a forward motion.

When you make a mistake, instead of focusing on it and beating yourself up, do what you can to fix the problem, and move on.

However, if a person or situation no longer serves you, step up and remove yourself or them. Forgiving someone isn't easy, even when they are trying to be better. It is extremely difficult to forgive someone who keeps hurting you. You can forgive someone, but that doesn't mean you have to allow damaging behavior. If someone is unable to stop their cycle of hurting you or those around you, they'll also have to become part of the past.

Step 2. Know thyself. Implement boundaries

Sabrina: I've always said, "GOD will handle them. Let me handle me." Decide what works for you and what doesn't and then abide by those rules. The desired peace and harmony you require for yourself is a standard you set. Your high vibrations for yourself dictate what you allow in and out of your life. If you know a person or situation is toxic and negative, don't allow them or it in your space. The power of NO is necessary. You will attract who you are. When you truly forgive, the heaviness will dissipate. When you truly forgive, the disorder and disharmony in your life will go away. People are people; some will never change. You change but remember: It's not about what happened to you; it's how you respond to what has happened. Rebuild your relationship with yourself.

Step 3. Avoid going to sleep angry; stop being MAD

Sabrina and Kenny: This can be difficult. We'd love to meet the person who has mastered this concept. Studies have shown that when you drift off to sleep, your subconscious mind controls everything that happens in your body. The subconscious mind creates your reality, depending on how you think and perceive.

When you sleep peacefully, you align your body and mind with the source of creation. One of the easiest ways to sleep peacefully is by listening to affirmations and visualizing what you want. This can allow you to let go of whatever happened during the day, which is a huge part of forgiveness. Try it next time. Instead of going to bed mad, release the anger. Much success happens with this discipline.

This is many times easier said than done. We have failed at this many times during our 30-year marriage. As the old saying goes, if you knew better, you would do better. Age and wisdom teach you much in life. You think about the times when you wasted days being mad. We also believe couples must weather the storms the best way they know how. You learn by doing. Some of our greatest battles in our marriage we did go to bed mad, and the feeling was of great pain -- the distance, the silence, and anger created was not the feeling that could sustain the marriage, so we worked to fix it.

Step 4: Take responsibility of your life

Sabrina: Change the way you perceive others, and your potential will be unlimited. Yes, in life, we will be treated unfairly. People will do you wrong whether on your job, with a lover, or a business deal, just to name a few. At some point in life, there will be major disappointments. Don't give others the power over your life to make you happy or sad, successful or unsuccessful. Own your power. Shift your focus from them to you. Don't blame another person or entity for your own wellbeing.

Find testimonies and read books about people who chose to turn their real-life living hell into heaven on earth. When I hosted a radio show, we had a man who served 22 years and 9 months in prison. He said every day he was incarcerated; his daily goal was to get better. Now that he's out, he has a successful trucking company and is living his best life. That started with his decision to not look backwards but to work towards building himself up every day and focus on the future. He shifted his mental energy to manage his thoughts and emotions, realizing that no one has the power to make you feel or do anything without your consent. By doing this, you'll easily master yourself and avoid blaming others for what is or isn't in your life.

Step 5. Avoid trying to control it all

Sabrina: I learned in an addiction support group years ago that I didn't cause it (the affliction), I can't control it, and I can't cure it. Give up the thought of control. This was a lesson that has helped me in many areas of my life.

As humans, we believe we can fix everything. This is especially difficult with other people. Avoid activities or thoughts that revolve around making decisions for capable people. Their decisions are their own; no matter how much you believe you'd do it better; you can't live their lives for them.

Parenting young adults has been probably one of our greatest challenges. Allowing young people to grow, make mistakes, and figure it out can be tough on parents. I often remind myself that our parents also had to grow through it with us. Even when our parents had the answers, self-discovery was always the better teacher.

Control what you can: your thoughts, your opinions, your actions. You will be much happier navigating life in that space, and your frustrations will decrease significantly. We don't know what tomorrow holds, but we do know who holds tomorrow. Trust in that. There are few certainties in life.

Step 6. Let Go and Let God

Sabrina: Letting Go and Letting God is certainly easier said than done. How many times have we let go and grabbed it back? I once saw a T-shirt that said, "I'm going to let God fix it because if I fix it, I'm going to be in jail." God is better equipped to fight our battles than we are.

Allow God to take control of your life. We tend to hold on to and harbor Ill feelings for far too long. Those hardened thoughts cause us to mistrust, mistreat, and misplace relationships. People grow and change and deserve second chances. Be clear though: If their behavior does not improve and is not acceptable to you, it's totally ok to let the relationship GO! Abusive behavior in any form should not be tolerated. If you are not feeling capable to handle the situation alone, seek counseling.

Our favorite scriptures that remind us to Let Go and Let God:

- 1 Peter 5:7: Give all your worries and cares to God, for he cares about you.
- Philippians 4:6: Don't worry about anything; instead, pray about everything.

Tell God what you need and thank him for all he has done. Then you will experience God's peace, which exceeds anything we can understand. His peace will guard your hearts and minds as you live in Christ.

Stop fretting. Don't force the idea and/or outcome. Manage yourself, your affairs, and give the rest to God.

Step 7. Give up always being right

Kenny: Let's face it. It's human nature to always want to be right. Nobody wants to be wrong. Instead of getting frustrated that everyone should have listened to you, work to replace that desire with peace and harmony. Stop focusing on what the other person is doing wrong and less on whether what you are doing or saying is right. Keeping track of who is right and wrong consistently is exhausting.

While it's natural to be filled with anger when someone does something wrong or when you could do it better, it's important to control your thoughts and emotions in those times. When you see yourself getting irritated, angry, or frustrated, remind yourself to own your emotions. Do not give ownership to anybody else.

Step 8. Embrace the difficult days

Sabrina and Kenny: "What doesn't kill you makes you stronger" comes from an aphorism of the 19th century German philosopher Friedrich Nietzsche. It has been translated into English and quoted in several variations but is generally used as an affirmation of resilience.

Relationships—both personal and professional— take work. They are not easy to create and or maintain. They are an investment. You must fight for what you believe in. The difficult days will grow you. You will learn much about yourself, and if the work put into the relationships allow individuals to get better, the bond should become stronger.

Draw strength from the experiences. If you don't see a light at the end of the tunnel and there is no betterment on the horizon, you must be astute and make the wise choice in moving forward. Embrace your own struggle every day. Learn from it and always work to do better. As you improve, let go and continue to grow, believing that every day can be better than the last.

Step 9. Express your feelings

Sabrina: It's ok, actually healthy, to talk about your feelings. Talking about your feelings will not only help you deal with a troubling situation but will also promote your mental health.

Talking about your feelings validates that what you are experiencing is real and means something to you. If you're upset over something, it's because you care about it. Ignoring that feeling would be invalidating to your experience and your values. By recognizing and seeking to understand your feelings, you'll learn what's important to you and be able to live a more fulfilling life in line with your values.

Do not suppress your thoughts. Talk it out. Women tend to express easier than men, but we can all learn to do this. When you open up, you encourage others to open up as well. At the end of the day, you realize the same problems that you have might be the same problems others are having. You might be able to help them, and/or they might be able to help you.

If you are not used to opening up, take small steps. The more comfortable you are, the easier this process will be for you. You can't fix what you are not willing to talk about.

Step 10. Ask for help

Sabrina and Kenny: Put fear and pride aside and get help. There are many people who are great at listening who are experts in this area, teaching one to forgive. You do not live on an island. If you do, you don't have to be isolated. Don't let the weight of unforgiveness bury you. Seek a support group or a counselor. Sometimes we need a guiding light to move us through the darkness. Remain hopeful. Know that your feelings, the circumstances, and/or situations are temporary, not permanent. Once we move ourselves through a situation, it is never as bad as it once was.

LEAVE THE JUDGMENT TO GOD

Kenny: My parents' divorce was hard. Seeing my family fractured and torn apart was hurtful. I was the last kid home (the baby boy); my brothers were at college. I feel like my parents put me in the middle of grown-up stuff. They divorced in high school, and I remember them coming to my wrestling matches, sitting on separate sides of the gym. For me, it was division; it was me having to pick sides. It was uncomfortable.

I had to make time for both after the match, listen to both sides of the conversation and be careful not to be biased toward one or the other. My job was to wrestle well, to stay as neutral as I could, and to be fair to both parents. At some point, I matured and decided it was not my responsibility to be the peacemaker for their life choices.

As I look back on the 1996 Olympics in Atlanta, where I was competing in my 3rd Olympic Games, I realize now how I was distracted by family matters. My brothers were having issues, and I was still dealing with my parents' divorce. I felt like I was being pulled in many different ways.

I didn't know how much I was bothered by it all until years later. I didn't compete well in Atlanta, and I could blame my family members, but I take full responsibility for not being my best. In order to figure out which parts of my performance I could control, I had to forgive my family for bringing so many concerns to me at a critical time in my career.

There was another time in my younger years that I still think about when I had to forgive my dad. I loved playing football in high school, but my dad made me quit when I was a junior. He told me I had to choose wrestling and could not play football anymore. He wanted me to focus on the sport that was going to afford me a college education. He thought I was too small to play football and didn't want me to get hurt.

I also had to forgive myself for being a rebel in reaction to his decision. I was a good player. My team was counting on me. I was a captain, an impact player, and I believed my leadership would lead us to a state championship. My coaches, the players, myself -- we were all disappointed. I felt as if I was letting the team down. I was trying to keep peace in house, and I didn't want to cause anymore arguments or confusion, so I reluctantly agreed with my dad's decision. I was upset and tried to stay away from home as much as possible. I was disappointed, and I started making bad decisions, drinking more, and doing recreational drugs. It was painful.

Knowing what I know now, you can't run from your problems. That wasn't the best way to deal with my frustrations, however, it ate at me. I knew I wasn't playing football in college. I understood that my focus was wrestling, but I believed I could do two sports well.

Our team got beat in the second-round playoffs in overtime to Oklahoma City Douglass High School. I still wonder if I had been on that team if we would have won State.

I forgave myself and my dad and used my energy to focus on wrestling. I went on to win four state titles and began my life's career. When you are not forgiving, it blocks progress and your ability to focus on your future in terms of goals and aspirations. It also dulls your creativity and overall mindset. When you don't forgive, it invites bitterness to creep in and you become envious, which is unhealthy for you physically and mentally.

As I forgave, it opened up my heart, released pressure, doubt, and anxiety. I began to pray, let go of pride, and better understood my dad was wanting to do what he thought was best for me and my future.

The journey is all a part of life's experiences. As you grow through hard things, you learn valuable lessons and those lessons learned I'm now able to teach my own children. These experiences mold you. You learn what to do and what not to do.

If you don't forgive, you can never be the best version of yourself. The deadly sin of unforgiving keeps you from loving yourself and others. Forgiveness is a humbling experience that allows you to see a situation for what it is. When you are a believer, your faith allows you to forgive. You can leave the judgment to God.

Notes/Reflections

FUN

Kenny and Sabrina: We work hard to play hard. We realized early on in the marriage that we must have a balance. I've been building my career in sales for 34 years; Kenny has been coaching for 30 years. We _do people_ for a living: coach them, build them, talk to them, get the best out them. That job can be all-encompassing. We love what we do, so we could do it 24/7, and it's become a part of our beings. But it's important to turn our work off. Shut it down. We have found all work and no play makes for boredom... and a dull life.

Our career demands much from us, physically and mentally. It's been important over the years to have fun and to refuel, to take time to step away from the business and come back to it, to have fresh eyes, and a deep passion to grow other people and ourselves in our respective careers.

Research has shown that couples who sustain a sense of mutual playfulness with each other tend to work out the issues in their relationships much better than those who are really serious. We find this to be absolutely true. If it wasn't for our laughter in the middle of an argument, I'm not sure we'd be here to write this book. Humor and play have gotten us through many serious situations in our life and in every area of our lives including our marriage, parenting, business, and all else. We work to make light of ourselves and the ordeal. When life gets too big, we have learned not to stress excessively and to give it to God.

We are compatible in that both of us have a light-hearted, upbeat personality. We both see the sunny side of things, always believing things will work out. We are eternal optimists. We love life! We love laughter! The Mondays are always up for a good time.

ADULTS SHOULD PLAY TOO

Adults play for many important reasons: building community, keeping the mind sharp, and keeping close the ones you love. When you don't play, there could be serious consequences. When people are serious all the time, they are not fun to be around. We have found that when you don't laugh, have fun, find joy in your work and life, life is less fulfilling.

There are many benefits of adults having fun, which include increased creativity, productivity, and feelings of well-being.

Sabrina: I have built a direct sales business that has been very fun over the years. All of my business conferences always include a good DJ, wonderful parties, and celebrations. I celebrate women to success. So yes, there is a lot of applauding, positive vibes given, high fives awarded, and an ultimate good time. I have made it my business to live with high vibrational energy. The days I'm lacking, Kenny has it and encourages me to get it. We are good for each other and know how to keep our energy high, which makes for a fun living environment.

You are a living energy field. Research shows your body is composed of energy producing particles, each of which is in constant motion. So, like everything and everyone else in the universe, you are vibrating and creating energy.

Vibrational energy experts claim that certain emotions and thought patterns like acceptance, peace, and joy create high-frequency vibrations, while other feelings and moods such as anger, despair and fear vibrate at a lower rate. When you are fun, people want to be around you because your vibrations are high. If you want to live at a higher vibration, it has been suggested to work on breath work, meditation, gratitude, generosity, and diet.

Connect with nature! Get outside! Did you know that interacting with nature lowers stress, lowers blood pressure, reduces fatigue, reduces cortisol levels and may lower your risk of cardiovascular and respiratory diseases?

What do you do for fun? No matter your budget, find the fun. Low budget fun might include going to a museum, aquarium, or zoo. As a family, we love family outings. Other things to do is to take a long drive on a nice day. Enjoy a picnic in the park with friends. Attend local music festivals. Put yourself in spaces that are uplifting, happy and jovial.

Join a book club! I was a member of a book club for years when I lived in Boston. There were 12 women in my reading circle, and each month, we would take a turn hosting the group. I looked forward to our monthly gatherings for fellowship and to discuss the book. Sometimes, we would read local authors and invite the author in to share.

Catch a movie, play, or watch a game. Go cheer somebody on. Volunteer. Giving always feels good. Visit the farmer's market or go thrift shopping; it's always fun to find deals.

Fun is celebrating victories with family and reminiscing with old friends. Our family played lots of games. We are competitive and like to win, whether we are playing cards, tennis, pool, or ping pong.

KENNY REMEMBERS

The year I won the Gold medal was the same year Barry Sanders won the Heisman Trophy at Oklahoma State University. I was out of season. Barry was too, and every once in a while, I'd go play basketball at the university's recreation room to get a sweat in and stay in shape. Well, Barry and I just happened to meet up at the court this night and we were on opposite teams. We matched up, and we were guarding each other. We were playing, going back and forth, up and down the court. I'm 5' 10" and Barry is about 5' 8". I turn around, and Barry jumps up, and I find myself looking at the bottom of his shoes. He was dunking on me. I was amazed he could get up that high.

That was fun playing him in basketball, talking trash, teasing each other, declaring who was the better athlete. Sports, recreational or professional, is fun for me.

LAUGHTER

Learn to laugh and hang out with fun people who love to laugh. The endorphins that are released when you laugh makes you feel better. The laughter creates energy. I have surrounded myself with a circle of people, friends, and family members who laugh with me and at me. Laughter is good for the soul. It allows you to drift from the problems of the world and gives you a release on life. Treasure the people in your world you can always count on for laughter.

TRAVEL

Sabrina: We have been blessed with travel over the years. We have traveled to over 40 countries, experiencing new cultures. Travel is one of the best ways to enhance personal growth. It enables you to do things outside your normal routine. Disrupting your normal routine is important to establishing fun. When you travel, you step out of your comfort zone to try new things, explore new food, and breathe a different air. This gives you a sense of freedom and independence. Traveling has been key for our human happiness, the time for us to unwind, and relax.

Kenny has traveled the world with his wrestling career. He has competed many times in Russia, Iran, and Turkey.

In my sales career, we have been awarded incredible incentive trips around the world. So many good times on this journey with amazing people who love getting all they can out of life.

Our favorite trips include climbing the Great Wall of China in Beijing and then having a private picnic with the Great Wall as our backdrop; there was a live band and the best Chinese food we have ever eaten. The Great Wall of China is one of the greatest sights in the world. The winding path over rugged country and steep mountains delivered breathtaking views.

We love Switzerland. This was my very first

international trip in 1999. I traveled there when I was 8 months pregnant. My doctor advised me not to go. My grandmother, who lived to be 102, said go, and told me, "The worst thing that could happen was to have a Swiss baby." So we went. My doctor gave me meds to slow down labor, just in case.

We had a blast in Switzerland, our favorite cities being Bern and Lausanne. Switzerland is lush and green. Clean and serene. Very peaceful. Every one minds their own business it seems.

One day, some friends had toured the Olympic Museum in Lausanne, Switzerland earlier in the day. They excitedly ran back to the hotel to tell us, "Guess who we saw in the museum?" Yes, they said there was a great Kenny Monday exhibit. This museum houses permanent and temporary exhibits relating to sports and the Olympic movement. We hurried over to the museum to see for ourselves. It was beautifully built and quite informative. We had no knowledge of this museum before we traveled. Kenny felt a great sense of pride being celebrated all the way in Switzerland in such a grand way. Of course, this has been a travel highlight for us over the years.

The flight back home was almost 14 hours! I was carrying my third child, and the other two came late, so I figured I would be just fine, and I was. We came back home to the USA with time to spare. Quincy, our youngest son, was born 7 days later. Now that was fun!

The Amalfi Coast is a stretch of coastline in southern Italy overlooking the Tyrrhenian Sea and the Gulf of Salerno. It is located south of the Sorrentine Peninsula and north of the Cilentan Coast. Just writing about this place brings back great memories. It is the most beautiful place I've ever laid eyes on. We had a private driver take us along the coastline, and I felt like I was in a dream. This place is sexy! I love everything about it-- the fashion, the food, the phenomenal architecture, the beautifully brightly painted pink, purple, yellow and blue villas tucked away in the mountains. I think everybody deserves to live this way.

We rented a villa for a week, with a huge veranda overlooking the sea. We wanted to get the authentic experience of the locals, so we took the local bus to the market. Navigating the tight turns and hills was an adventure. The charming towns, local vendors, warm waters, and pristine beaches welcomed us on the Amalfi

Coast. We celebrated my birthday—a great celebration. I will never forget how the champagne flowed, and we toasted to the fun, unforgettable times.

Santorini Greece is one of the Cyclades islands in the Aegean Sea and is the most famous of all Greek islands and a number one summer destination worldwide. The beauty of this island is incomparable to any other in the world. The amazing caldera formed by the volcanic eruption centuries ago resulted in the most amazing sea views a human eye can ever see.

Go to Santorini just for the pictures! OMG, the luxury whitewashed houses perched on caldera cliffs with extraordinary views to the Aegean Sea creates a fairy tale backdrop. This island is one of the top wedding destinations in the world.

We bought lots of white linen there. The shop owners were quite kind and encouraged us to spend lots of money, of course I did the flying dress photo shoot!

In our home, raising children, we worked to create a fun lively household. One could always find a party at the Mondays. There was always something to celebrate: straight As, a great wrestling season, a birthday, a holiday -- just give us a reason. It was family time to celebrate one another's success. When our kids were younger, every summer in late July or early August, we would take a family vacay to Cabo San Lucas.

We owned a time share at this beautiful resort. Our first condo was a two-bedroom on the first floor. It was the best sleep I've ever had because you could hear the crashing of the waves so closely.

As the kids got older, we needed more space and got a three-bedroom penthouse with a huge hot tub on the deck. We certainly got our money's worth. We had some good times over the years. It was our time to refuel and reconnect as a family, a time to appreciate the kids for doing the right thing. It was a time to get away from the daily grind and enjoy one another.

Cabo was easy to get to. It was direct travel from Dallas, only about a two-and-a- half-hour flight. We would get the tickets early and look for the best deals for a family of five. We did this for 5 years. Our oldest was 8 when we started and our youngest was 4.

Being empty nesters now, our children are young adults, living their lives. It's now just us, so fun is at the top of our list. We believe at this stage and age in life, we have earned every ounce of freedom and fun.

Finding Fun Even in a Pandemic

The pandemic slowed our Fun-do-meter down quite a bit. Fun deprivation is a thing, and we had to get creative. The fun things that were done on a regular basis became a thing of the past, a recollection of distant thoughts in the recesses of our brains. World class travel, big sporting events, fine dining, concerts, hosting family reunions...oh how we missed our normal fun in our lives. Never to be taken for granted again.

The pandemic paused many activities causing our lives, and everybody else's lives, to stand still. It put a dull on our shine, so we did lots virtually, from weddings to birthday parties to dance parties and unfortunately funerals; so many lives were lost.

We were grateful for technology to be able to connect with friends and family in meaningful ways.

The fun, creative virtual experiences made us feel alive. They renewed our zest for life and gave us energy. Gathering with fun friends and family who are optimistic, love to laugh, are winners and not whiners make all the difference.

Fun can be as simple as family, good attitudes, good food and good music! In the pandemic, we had house parties with immediate family members. The first year, all the kids were back home, and we quarantined together. Sydnee was able to work from our home. Kennedy was doing online school at UNC, where we lived in Chapel Hill. Quincy, our youngest, took a gap year from Princeton to give the world time to get itself together and heal from COVID 19.

DJ Nice, who became famous for pulling hundreds of thousands together on Instagram by playing the best music and connecting all of us who were home bound became a staple in our house! Music alters the mood. We were grateful for the time. Even though time appeared to be standing still, we found a way to create a fun environment.

FAMILY PETS BRING FUN!

Pets bring lots of fun to the family. Before I got married, I wasn't really a dog person; Kenny has always loved dogs. When we first got together, he had a chow named Cheeba and a Shar Pei named Luke. He was quite slobbery. They were his dogs, and I was the newcomer to the family. Cheeba was very territorial.

As time went on, the dogs got away. Kenny tells the story that he went away to train at a wrestling camp, came home, and I did something with his dogs. I don't remember the story going that way. I remember them running away or somebody stealing them. Long live those two.

It's no secret that dogs make us happier people. They provide a lot of fun. Dogs have served as man's best friend and worked alongside us for thousands of years. The loyal companionship and unconditional love of dogs has been known about throughout human history. A study recently revealed that pet owners have greater self esteem, are more physically fit, less lonely, more socially outgoing, and have healthier relationship styles than non–pet owners.

As our family grew, our first family dog was a great Pyrenees, a mountain dog known to guard livestock. He was such a great family pet and protector. We were coming from our friend's, Wil Haygood's book signing in Dallas. Wil is a world-renowned writer and had written a book on Sammy Davis Jr. The book signing was a success, we had a great time, and while driving home, we saw a family selling puppies on the side of the road. One of the kids convinced us to stop; it was a leisurely Saturday afternoon, and we were in no rush. The cutest puppies ever were in the back of this truck. Of course, the kids— 2, 4 and 8—had to have one of them. We all picked the whitest dog with no markings on him. We bought him for $25. After pondering different names, Quincy, our youngest son, named him Sammy, after Sammy Davis Jr.

We had no idea what kind of dog he was until we went home and researched him, finding that he was a Great Pyrenees mixed with a Husky. Kenny discovered that this dog would grow to be more than 100 lbs. We took him to the vet on that Monday, and they confirmed he was going to be big. Sure enough, over the first few months, he was gaining 15–20 pounds a month. Sammy became a great friend to the family. He was a joy and played with the kids well. He was with us for 8 years, until the summer of 2012. He died of cancer, right before we left for the London Olympics.

Even small interactions with dogs cause the human brain to produce oxytocin, a hormone often referred to as the cuddle chemical. Oxytocin increases feelings of relaxation, trust, and empathy while reducing stress and anxiety.

We missed having a family dog, so we started researching different breeds. We visited family in Washington, DC, and they had a whacky, loveable Goldendoodle. We fell in love with that breed. Kenny started talking to people and identified a breeder in Texas. We were living in Oklahoma at the time. He told us he was expecting a litter in October, and we could pick the puppy up in December. We thought, *yay, a puppy for Christmas.*

Well, it was time to pick up our new puppy, and Kenny was away on business. This dog was not $25; he was $1800. My sister, Regina, drove with me to Texas to pick up the puppy. He constantly cried on the highway in his crate. I couldn't take it, so my sister held him for four hours until we got home. The kids fell in love with him instantly. It was always fun coming up with the family pet name. We were excited about the upcoming Rio Olympics in 2016, in Rio de Janeiro, so we named him Rio.

He was a great new puppy. He loved to play, was easy to train, and blended easily into our family. He has been a trooper, easily adapts to his environment, and has moved a lot in the 10 years we've had him. Rio was born in Texas, moved to Oklahoma, then to Florida, then back to Texas, then to North Carolina, Ohio, and now Maryland. Yes, Mondays on the move! Kenny's coaching career has moved us to wherever the next best team is, but Rio hasn't complained one bit. He is a perfect fit.

Golden doodles are amazing dogs -- part golden retriever, part standard poodle. Those two breeds are in the top 5 smartest dog categories, so we knew we couldn't go wrong with dog intelligence.

Dogs have provided great fun for our family. If you don't have a family pet of some sort, we encourage you to get one. They need you, and you need them.

ENJOY YOURSELF!

Adults need to play. George Bernard Shaw, an Irish playwright once said, "We don't stop playing because we grow old; we grow old because we stop playing." These ten tips have helped us add more fun and play to our life.

1. Decide what fun means.
2. Add fun in even at work or working out.
3. Put fun on the calendar plan for it.
4. Give up fun guilt. YOU deserve it!
5. Create fun, using puzzles, card games, field trips.

6. Find fun people to hang out with.

7. Find babies and toddlers; they bring joy. Go to friends and relatives' homes that have babies.

8. Travel; expand your five senses.

9. Get out of a normal routine and mix things up.

10. Know when your fun fuel tank is running low and fill up. Life is to be well lived; live it out loud with laughter and fun.

Notes/Reflections

FEARLESSNESS

As Franklin D. Roosevelt stated during his 1933 presidential inauguration, "There is nothing to fear but fear itself." If you can embrace that idea and become fearless in all aspects of your life, it becomes synonymous with unstoppable. What would you do in your life if you were fearless?

Fear is limiting, skews our perception, makes us feel like victims, helpless and hopeless, erodes trust, and brings out the worst in us. Just think about when you have been fearful. I'm sure you can relate to these feelings.

Sabrina: Living in fear is also simply unhealthy. It brings dis-ease, which can cause disease. My grandmother used to say, "You are going to worry yourself sick!" I now understand the phrase.

I learned to overcome fear while traveling the world (to over 40 countries) for business and pleasure, moving

8 times in the US and not knowing if it would work out or not. I couldn't overanalyze all the *what if it doesn't work out.* I just had to believe that it would.

I was born in Oklahoma, attended college in Tennessee, moved to Massachusetts for grad school, got married, returned to Oklahoma, started a family, then we moved to Texas. Kenny took a job offer back in Oklahoma, we then moved to Florida for another opportunity that didn't work out great, and we found ourselves back in Texas. Another great coaching opportunity for Kenny came about and took us to North Carolina, then to Ohio, and now Maryland. Many have asked us if we are a military family because we have moved so much, and the answer is always no, but the life of a coach is quite similar. You go where the teams are.

I focused on being fearless in the pursuit of my dreams. Most people will never understand your path. That is why I have always been clear to make the best decisions for me, not allowing other people's opinions or fears dictate my life.

Being an entrepreneur, you must take risks. You can't stay in a safe place. There has been fear in my career, going for a big goal, approaching strangers, and experiencing rejection is a definite fear. Failure is also part of the plan. It's important to have a strong mentality to overcome fear, as fear resides within each of us. Build up enough confidence to be strong enough to overcome your fears.

In life, I have found you must not be afraid to take chances. Because my business allows me to build wherever I am, I've been able to create customers and new team members in all states. I remember when I first decided to build my business internationally. People's opinions and reactions could have scared me into not pursuing a global presence. There were so many questions and statements like, "You are going without your husband? Kenny is letting you go to South America alone? I hear those places are dangerous, don't get kidnapped." However, I did my own research on the areas of interest, and I'm grateful that I decided to take that chance. I've been able to diversify my organization in several regions, even countries, because I was willing to feel the fear and *do it anyway*. I now have a global business in Brazil, Colombia, Spain, Mexico, and Canada.

MASTERING FEAR

Fear can be a good thing, as long as you learn to use it and learn to master it. Make fear work for you not against you. Fear will push you out of your comfort zone. Fear is a normal emotion. You can feel it and move around it. As a competitor, the thought of losing made both of us better. (Kenny trained consistently, worked harder, and kept the vision of his opponents close. Sabrina learned to face risk and grow through it.)

Here are key points we have adopted so fear doesn't trap us.

EMBRACE FEAR

Fear is a part of your life. People, places, and things will make us uncomfortable.

Be ready for adversity because it is coming your way. Identify it. Name the fear. Look fear in the face. Put a game plan in place to not let fear rule your life. Do something about it.

Now that you have come to terms with the emotion of fear, what will you do with it? Do not sit with it or in it.

OVERCOMING FEAR

In order to overcome fear, you have to enroll in fighting it. Whenever you embark upon someone, something new or different, you may be uncomfortable. That's normal but preparation and putting the work in builds confidence. If you know a challenge is coming, get ready for it. Learn what it will take to overcome it and do the work. There are no shortcuts.

EXPERIENCE FEAR

Put yourself in fearful situations. The fear will lessen the more you work to overcome the fearful emotion. One of our best friends was petrified of public speaking. Her new sales career forced her to speak often, in front of larger audiences. The more she spoke, the more the fear started to dissipate. Now she is an incredible public speaker, and she even surprises herself at how at ease she is with, at one point, was terrifying for her.

ENJOY THE GROWTH

Life has a way of stretching us. Overcoming fear brings growth, and you should respect the process. Your mind is like a rubber band; there are many things in life that will stretch you! You should always put yourself in a position to learn and grow, becoming the best version of yourself. Confidence and belief will be sure to follow.

FACING FEAR

Kenny: I learned to overcome fear early in my life, when I was 5. After my first wrestling match, I realized being afraid wasn't beneficial. I quickly became fearless. This mentality shaped me as a young boy. You can beat me in other areas; however, I was determined that you were not going to beat me on me being fearful. It fared well for me over the years. No way could I have achieved the level of success I have by being fearful. I was taught that, now I coach it.

In my sport, I learned early on to wrestle the body not the name. As a young wrestler, I worked to win, but it can be hard to focus on your own performance if your competitor is a big name. I was lucky to learn early on that the name didn't matter.

When we step into the ring, we're all just people. And people—any person—can get pinned. The more I wrestled, the more victories I accrued. My name grew in the sport, and soon enough, I had a big name. I remember wrestling good kids who wouldn't compete because they were afraid of my name. I could sense that, and they were beat before we got on the mat.

As we wrestled, they realized they could compete with me, but it was too late. By then, I had already scored 10 points or so, or I would have them pinned. At that point, the match was over. Don't be that person, walking into a situation scared. You must give yourself the best opportunity to win, and it's hard to win afraid.

Growing up as the youngest, I had to hold my own to get to hang with my older brothers. If my brothers put me in the game, I had to show up, fearless. The older boys were bigger, stronger, and faster, but no matter what, I had to be ready to compete. If they threw me the ball, I had to hustle and catch it, and run like crazy. I always worked to prove to myself and to my big brothers that I was capable and able. I never wanted them to think that I couldn't hold my own. I did what it took to measure up. I didn't want the opportunity denied being with the big boys. That circle boosted my skill set and confidence.

I attended Robert Frost elementary, and I was at Dunbar elementary a lot because my mom worked at the school. I spent a lot of time on both playgrounds. There were some tough kids at both schools. You couldn't have fear on the playground or you would get bullied. You couldn't afford to be afraid. I developed a tough mentality early on, if only to survive the playgrounds. I wasn't afraid of anybody on the playground. *You mess with Boo, you had a fight on your hands, and not an easy fight.*

I do recall losing one fight. It was the only fight *I've ever lost in my life*, and I will never forget it. I was in the fourth grade. My classmate, Benny, told me a kid jumped him. I knew it wasn't right, and I wanted to help him do something about it. I confronted the kid. I remember he was a big, strong kid, always picking on others, smelled like pee, probably flunked a couple of times—yeah, you know the type. Well, when I approached him, we started scuffling, and he threw a punch. It landed, and he gave me a black eye.

As I write this, it still gives me a feeling of uneasiness. The fight was early in the day, so I had to walk around school with a black eye all day with all the questions: "What happened?" The answer was short: "I got beat up."

The longer the day went on, the more revenge I wanted. I knew the kid walked home from school, and I knew the route. I patiently waited for him behind the tree, and at just the right time, I jumped from behind the tree and got my revenge.

Word spread to the teachers that we were fighting in the field, up the street from the school. They ran down and broke up the fight.

We both got in trouble. We got a paddling from the principal. He came back and apologized, and I never had any more problems from him again. The score had been settled.

Those experiences taught me early on not to be fearful, and I can't recall being fearful of an opponent in my wrestling career. I trained my brain to embrace fearlessness. Mastering my mindset early in life has been key to my success. I never went into a match thinking I couldn't win. I thought I would win every match. Even when I wasn't good enough, maybe, I thought I was better than I was. Even if my opponent had a better record, I was counting on them having a bad day.

In 1986–1987, the 1988 Olympic trials were quickly approaching, and I knew I was behind my competition.

I was coming from not placing in the World team trials the prior year, having to face some of the best Russian wrestlers in the 165 lb. weight class and Dave Schultz, the defending world champ from the USA.

I didn't fear the other wrestlers. I knew fear wasn't in my best interest. But I did fear not having enough time to jump levels in my training to compete with the best of the best in the world and win. I used that fear to train harder and smarter. I knew I simply wasn't good enough. My total focus was to get better to be ready for the 1988 Olympics.

However, I also feared my opponents' sponsor, John du Pont. He was powerful and persuasive enough to keep me from my destiny.

The wrestling community is relatively small. Everybody keeps up with who is winning and who is losing. In competition at this level, the stakes are high. Politics are involved and people are paid to maneuver the system. What I feared is what I couldn't control. I feared the system that John du Pont—the now deceased convicted murderer and philanthropist—controlled. An heir to the du Pont family fortune, from one of the richest families in the US, this man had a big influence because of the money he provided to athletes and to USA Wrestling.

Du Pont's number one wrestler was Dave Schultz. He wrestled for du Pont's acclaimed, world-renowned club, Foxcatcher. Schultz was my biggest competitor. I had to beat him in 1988 to make my first Olympic team. However, the next Olympic cycle, du Pont was determined to have me beat one way or the other.

In 1989, I had to pull out of the US Open tournament because I bit my tongue and had to have 15 stitches. Because I didn't place in that tourney, because of my injury, I had to wrestle 15 matches to make the world team in 1989. It was a difficult feat. But I did it.

In 1990, I was wrestling well. I had made it to my finals match in the US Open in Las Vegas. I went to the table to see if my weight class had been released, and they said there was one more match before it would be released. The rule then was that the athletes got 90 minutes to make weight after your weight class had been released. It was 8:30 pm, and I was a couple of pounds over my goal weight, so I went to get the weight off. I came back at 9:30 pm to weigh in, and they said I was a minute late. The weigh-ins had shut down at 9:30. I was not allowed to weigh in and was disqualified from the tournament. According to the 90-minute rule, the weighin time would have been 10 pm. I protested the ruling— to no avail, and du Pont threatened to take his funding if they let me wrestle. I couldn't get help from anyone. It felt like the system was rigged.

This tournament was critical. The top 3 athletes at the US Open placed for the world team trials. It was critical that I won that tournament because the number one guy is at the top of the ladder. All of my hard work at this tournament now discounted and discarded.

Being unfairly pulled out of competition almost made me quit the sport. However, my relentless will to win, not letting fear sabotage me from my dreams, prevailed. I couldn't let fear of a rich, powerful man and the system deter me from becoming all that I could be. At this point, I really thought about quitting the sport. I simply didn't know how I could compete with the powers that be.

With much prayer, consoling, and consulting, I jumped back into training and decided to compete at the 1990 world team trials. I had a great tournament, but I lost my final match, the best 2 out of three in the finals match. I was out. I didn't make the 1990 world team.

With grit, fearlessness, and determination I came back and made the 1991 world team. I placed 2nd in the 1991 world championships and then made the Olympic 1992 team, winning the Silver medal for USA. I didn't win all of my matches, but I won many, because there was no fear, and I believed in myself. I'm grateful that I didn't let my fear keep me from my dreams.

Du Pont later died in prison while serving 30 years for the murder of Dave Schultz.

Fear can make you better. I learned how to make fear work for me not against me. Fear has been my motivator throughout the years, and I have passed that on to my own kids and the athletes I've coached.

FAITH FIGHTS FEAR

Sabrina: We all know fear stops many from achieving their dreams and our belief system is rooted in not being afraid to take risks. Prayer has always been our greatest go-to, finding scriptures that empower us and makes us stronger. The scripture we rely on most in overcoming fear is 2 Timothy 1:7: "For God has not given us a spirit of fear and timidity, but of power, love, and self-discipline." I have recited and meditated on this scripture so many times during times in my life when I was unsure and sometimes scared.

Many times, when going for a big goal, on one side of my brain, there is an angel hovering over me whispering, "You are the best, you can do it, you are well equipped." If God gave you the vision, He would give you the provision. And then there is the other side of the brain, devil with the pitchfork in his hand screaming, "You are no good! You can't! You don't! You will fail! Why even try? You are not good enough, so just settle."

Fear will come. Be ready. It's hard to live in fear and walk in greatness.

I prayed about my international journey; it was a dream of mine. I knew if I took God as my power partner, being as careful and conscientious as possible and not be gripped with fear, but full of faith, God would bless me with the desires of my heart, which is a thriving international business. I chose to step out on faith and leave fear behind. I've always preached to my children you won't know unless you go. It's not what is taught, it's *what is caught*. Go with your gut, believe in yourself. Go forth my friends; explore the world, do something you have never done before. Make fear take a back seat in your life.

Notes/Reflections

FINISH!

Sabrina: To finish something is to complete or bring it to a conclusion. Finishing feels good. Finishing well feels even greater. Think about the times you have finished a great meal, a class, or a degree at the university. I'm thinking now how elated I will feel when we finish this book!

Being a finisher grants you accolades and plaudits; it rewards you in many ways. Finishing gives you confidence, a sense of accomplishment. Finishing gives the necessary punctuation to a project—sometimes a comma, maybe a question mark or an exclamation point. There often lies the period when you are finished with a project and sometimes a relationship.

Finishing is a decision, finishing is a focus, finishing takes determination and dedication. It is being resolute in your understanding. If you don't finish, it leaves you in the coulda, shoulda, woulda club. Always wondering *what if?* When you leave something undone, you could live a life of regrets. If it's important, it's important to finish it. Finishers find their way in the BIDIA (But I Did It Anyway) club. Finishers are fulfilled. Finishers look for the next ring on the ladder to climb; it's hard to climb up the ladder when you don't complete a step.

To be a finisher, there must be positive self-talk and reinforcement to finish the job. Many times, there is coaching from others that creates self-esteem and confidence and eliminates or decreases self-sabotage. Empower yourself with an arsenal of books, music that moves you, sermons from your preacher, and conversations from loved ones that push you to the finish line. Always remember why you started the project so you can remember why you should finish it.

Kenny: The NCAA wrestling tournament is one of the greatest shows on Earth, especially if you are a wrestler, coach, parent, or fan. Thirty-three of the nation's best college wrestlers compete in a 3-day grueling tournament that will produce and honor the top eight wrestlers in 10 different weight categories. When the dust settles at the conclusion of the competition, the top eight place winners are considered All- Americans.

Most student athletes, if they are good enough and qualify, get four opportunities to compete in the prestigious NCAA tournament, affectionately referred to as "The Big Dance."

The 2022 NCAA wrestling season was our youngest son, Quincy's, third opportunity to become a national champion and earn All-American status. He wrestled for Princeton University. His first year as a true freshman, he got sick 3 days before the tournament started, never recovered, and went 0-2 and got beat out of the tournament. The next year, his sophomore season, Quincy had a strong and impressive year, earning the 5th seed leading into the NCAA tournament. Unfortunately, a week before the tournament was set to begin, COVID hit and shut down the season, cancelling the NCAA tourney, depriving the athletes from reaching their dreams of becoming true All-Americans. However, in title only, because Quincy was top 8 in the country, he was named All-American.

Fall 2022 -- that year was different. Quincy was now a junior in college and had matured a great deal since his freshman season. He was having an incredible year, compiling a record of 30-3, losing only to the No. 2, 3 and 4 seed in the NCAA tournament. Again, just like his sophomore season, Q was again voted the 5th seed going into this year's tournament at Little Caesars Arena in Detroit, Michigan. The Princeton team was highly motivated this year after not being able to compete the previous year. The Princeton Tigers team's motto of their 2022 season was "Unfinished Business." When the brackets were released a few days before the tournament started, Quincy and I had several conversations about his placement in the bracket and his path to a National Championship and being an all-American.

Kenny: Wrestling in the NCAA tournament 4 times myself, being a 3x finalist and NCAA Champion my senior year, I understood how the flow of the tournament worked. Q's goal from the beginning of the season was to win the National Championship. So, the focus was clearly to finish that goal on top of the podium. The game plan was to take each match one at a time and wrestle every match like it was the finals, never looking past the match that was in front of him. The NCAA tournament is always laced with upsets and performances that you've never seen all year.

In the quarter final match, Q was up against the No.

4 seed. This wrestler had beat him earlier in the season. Again, our message was clear: finish your matches strong and you will advance.

Quincy stormed into the NCAA finals, knocking off the 4th seed in the quarter final match and winning his semifinal match 3-2. Quincy won four straight matches earning a spot in NCAA finals against the No. 2 seed!

Quincy made history at Princeton University. For the first time ever, they had two NCAA wrestling finalists—him and his roommate, Patrick Glory, at 125 lbs.—competing for the NCAA championships. Only two other schools had multiple finalists that year, Michigan and Penn State.

The adrenaline was high. 20,000 fans filled the arena, and it was broadcast on ESPN TV. We were pumped. The tournament started with wrestlers competing on 8 different mats. We were now down to the one mat center stage. We had one more victorious finish to bring home the NCAA 157 lb. Championship. The preparation had been done; the plan was in place...

Our family was invited by ESPN to sit on the floor seats mat-side; they wanted us close to the action, to capture our every emotion, be it happy or sad. Going into the third and final period, the match was tied 2-2. The fans were screaming, ESPN cameras were everywhere, catching family sentiments and every wrestling move. Quincy lost the match in the finals. Disappointed for sure, but not derailed, finishing does not always give us our desired outcome, but it's important to **finish** what you start. Many people abandon their goals too easily. You must work with the end in mind and create finishing habits. Below are a few habits that we've found important for crossing the finish line.

KNOW WHAT YOU ARE STARTING

Be mindful of what you are embarking upon. Do the research. Don't make an emotional decision before you jump in; make a thoughtful decision. Value your time and energy. Time spent in one area is time away from another.

When embarking upon different projects or goals in life, you sometimes don't know what you are getting into until you are in it and then the necessary adjustments must be made. Sometimes you know what all is involved and sometimes, you don't.

Kenny: In 1987, I was enrolled at Oklahoma State University in Stillwater, Oklahoma. I was grinding in class and training hard to make my first USA Olympic team. The demands of my classroom work and the effort it took to make the 1988 Olympic team became quite challenging. As much as I thought I could make both work, it was difficult. I wrestled in one of the toughest Russian tournaments in 1987, placing 5th. I knew I had to get better. My training needed more time and focus. There was no way I was going to make that team at the level I was competing at. I came home and made the difficult decision to withdraw from school, to dedicate my full attention and time to my training. I knew I simply was not good enough to make the team; therefore, I had to change my effort and time given toward the goal. As I've mentioned, the decision was unpopular with my parents; they didn't understand why I needed to stop going to school to pursue my Olympic dreams and disagreed with my decision. They wanted me to continue with both, always reminding me if my plans didn't work out, I'd have my degree to fall back on. I understood their point; however, I also knew what was required of me to better myself in the sport, and I only had a short timeframe to prepare. The 1988 Olympic Games in Seoul, Korea, were quickly approaching.

Family support was important to me and once I made the decision, my parents better understood my position and encouraged me to give it my all. I was able to train wholeheartedly with no distractions, increasing my workouts, and also having additional time to study my opponents via film.

I went back to the same tournament in 1988 and won 10 straight matches, becoming one of only 11 Americans to win the legendary TBILISI tournament in Russia. It was that year that I also qualified to make the US Olympic team and win the Gold medal. Deviation from your Plan A is not necessarily a bad strategy; you must be comfortable with your thinking and with your Plan B. Know what you're getting into and have full confidence in that knowledge.

UNDERSTAND THE RESOURCES NEEDED

Write down what your project will take: time, money, people, education, and expertise. Who are the players and where will resources come from? Do you have what it takes to get the job done? It is one thing to start a thing and another to finish. A clear example is when you see new construction go up; the building is only halfway finished, and yet it is still sitting there partially built out 10 years later. Obviously, plans went awry, resources ran out. If you plan your resources and set out from the start with not just your needs but your requirements in mind, you are less likely to falter.

In 1995, one year before coming out of retirement and making my third USA Olympic team, for the 1996 Olympic Games in Atlanta, Georgia, I was approached to buy a Subway franchise and a gourmet coffee shop on the University Center at Tulsa college campus.

I was excited about the possibilities, but I knew my time was limited. To do this project, I needed the necessary resources to support this vision. It was a big investment of finances and time. Throughout my wrestling career, I've met many great people who have become great business partners and advisors. I sought much advice before I said yes to these business ventures. In establishing businesses in my hometown, I had name recognition and family support to help establish and maintain the operations. The location was key, with builtin traffic and offering goods and services that didn't exist on campus. It was not an easy undertaking. I learned a lot about myself, my business, and others during this time.

Entrepreneurship is certainly not for the faint at heart. Among the many resources needed for our businesses to thrive was a trusted team. A team that I could count on to make sure the doors were open, and the businesses ran efficiently in my absence. I was training for the 1996 upcoming Olympics in Phoenix, Arizona. I had to make sure the trained team, with my wife managing the businesses, represented my brand; my customers expected and deserved excellence. The team had to be self- starters and needed not to be micromanaged. Both businesses took manpower and financial investment. With the right human resources— especially my wife—they were able to run the businesses without me, allowing me to focus on training.

GIVE YOURSELF A REASONABLE TIMETABLE

When you take on a project, if you do not have a deadline, give yourself one. It is difficult to get any job done with no timeline. It's also important to work within the time that allows you an adequate period to properly do the job. I have found myself rushing through projects because I committed to a timetable that was unreasonable to start with.

Sabrina: In my direct sales business, I always seemed to be chasing the clock. We work with month-end deadlines to hit sales quotas. In sales, I find myself always desiring more time to hit goals. I am grateful for deadlines. They make you move toward the mark with a sense of urgency. I teach the people in my organization to front load their month. Instead of waiting and procrastinating to get a job done, **do it now**! Time really is our greatest asset. You use it or lose it. Once gone, you can never get it back. Give yourself ample time to successfully complete a project.

Over time, we are now professional movers. Many of our friends get frustrated with moving. Most have always lived in the same city and/or state, and maybe have moved once in their life. For us, we plan, prepare and understand the process. Make sure the appropriate time is allowed for a successful stress-free move. We hire a moving company 60-90 days in advance, contract the packers at least 2 months in advance. If cars need to be moved, contract them at least 4-6 weeks in advance.

With moving, we have found they get booked up quickly, and the frustration happens when what you need doesn't work with your schedule.

You can't expect great things to happen if you have not properly planned. You must know what the project entails, outline the details, and give yourself adequate time to finish strong. If not, you set yourself up for failure.

DON'T BE A PERFECTIONIST

It's great to have high expectations for yourself and others; however, many perfectionists never finish projects because they tend to overthink and focus on the results more than working the process. It's important to worry less and do more. Break tasks down into steps that you can manage. Stop being critical of yourself. Focus on what assets and skills you bring to the project as opposed to what you don't have.

Surround yourself with others who possess the skill set you are lacking.

For many families, a family split to take on a job living in a different state would not work, like when Kenny took the job at Oklahoma State University. But for us, it was imperfectly perfect. There were lots of imperfect dinners for the boys. They still fondly recall lots of beef patties and rice, very few veggies, lots of cereal, and stopping by the local gas station every day after school for a snack. We all made sacrifices as a family to make it work. We were clear this was a temporary season in life, and we would get through it.

Do the best you can, whenever you can, however you can.

COMMIT

When you are committed, you are in a black or white zone. There is no gray area. Your intentions are clear. If you are not 100 percent in, you are 100 percent out. Either something is worth 100 percent of your effort or it's not worth your effort at all. You must be committed to finish and be willing to do whatever it takes. No excuses allowed.

VISUALIZE THE RESULT

Create a mental picture of the finish line. How will you feel, who will you be with, how will you celebrate, what will life look like? When we visualize our desired outcome, we begin to see the possibility of achieving it. Keep the visual in your mind, on your wall, and in your planner. The image of completion encourages us to keep going.

When faced with splitting the family up when Kenny took the job with OSU, we knew it would be a short-term sacrifice and had to focus on the school yearend results. Our motivation was knowing that Sydnee's high school career would not be interrupted with Kenny's career move, and she would get to keep her high school routine with little disruption. Traveling to Italy for her student exchange program, she stayed with a sweet Italian family that housed her where she went to school with the locals and learned the language. That year was a clear benefit of finishing. She also learned that the end of one big finish is the beginning of the next.

FIND JOY IN THE JOURNEY

In the middle of the project, event, or whatever it is you are working on, the process can become tedious, tiring, uneventful, and at times flat out difficult. Create ways to lift your spirits. Take a break when needed and involve other people who bring a new perspective.

It's so important to enjoy the journey in your life's work. Time flies by, and we're so busy worrying about what we haven't done instead of what we're doing. Our progress is often impeded by roadblocks and life circumstances. Work to find peace in your purpose. Take breaks, take a walk, find beauty around you, pick a flower, enjoy the birds singing. Find some joy and peace in every part of your day. Get away in your mind – it can be watching your puppy play haphazardly instead of turning on the news. As a matter of fact, turn the news off. Turn on some music and dance as if no-one is watching; read uplifting, positive quotes; read scriptures that empower you; pick up the phone and call a friend who makes you laugh. It is important to take joy breaks throughout the day. Write in your journal and soak up the sunshine. Find it and bask in it, if only for a few minutes. Keeping a gratitude journal centers you and keeps you positive. Listen to yourself. Pause the push when necessary.

Opportunities that we are afforded broaden our horizons. Keep in mind that whatever you are creating and/ or developing is a privilege that many wish they had.

Our family's thought: most of the time, whatever we are embarking upon is something we chose to do, not something we have to do.

TRACK YOUR PROGRESS!

Tracking your progress as you finish a project is imperative. It gives you clarity on the status of different tasks and dictates where the most work is needed. Charting the details gives you a hard focus.

As human beings, we are built to want to reach the finish line. Our brain seeks the dopamine we get from crossing off tasks and checking the boxes. We like the word DONE! Tracking helps you stay committed to your work and helps you to feel good about being on a path of progress. Growth is nourished by encouragement. Small wins are motivators along the way, so don't ignore them. The little wins add up to the big wins! Recognizing the milestones give you an opportunity to reflect, reevaluate, and recharge.

I have earned the use of 16 pink Cadillacs in my 34-year career with Mary Kay Cosmetics, Inc., it has always been important during the qualification process to track progress and know the measurable benchmarks to achieve the desired success. The coveted pink trophy on wheels, as a sales director, is earned every two years. Tracking success was a must. If you didn't track, you could easily miss the mark. If you don't know where you are, you don't know how to grow.

The car can be tracked and earned every 2 years in a six-month period. I first break my numbers down quarterly and then look at the six-month totals. I create my work plan every week that led to the months and the months led to the qualifying quarters. All of my qualification periods were different based on the different people in my organization at the time. Earning the use of the many cars over the years kept me sharp and disciplined, always stretching me out of my comfort zone. The more cars I earned, the easier they became because I had a system, I understood the numbers, and I had confidence in my understanding of what was needed to get the job done. Clarity is key.

It's important to be honest with yourself throughout the process, giving yourself a thorough assessment of where the work needs to be done. Chart yourself along the way, making sure you are on track with your deadlines. The many goals I've set for myself in business over the years have given me the discipline to track other important things in life.

LET GO OF GUILT

If you miss the deadline or the project doesn't work out, you learn by doing. All experiences should give you an opportunity to grow and learn. Focus on the good that came out of the time invested. Don't waste effort feeling bad or being remorseful; use that time to regroup and move on.

You will find many good starters in our world -- people who have great ideas starting projects with great intentions, high enthusiasm, and a strong commitment. Then there is a bump in the road. The difficulty appears and the tools to get restarted begin to dwindle and the finish line becomes more distant. The belief in the project dissipates. This pattern of behavior, if not monitored, can become a bad habit that goes nowhere fast. It can lead to a road of starting and stopping and never finishing.

As we go through life, we tend to measure what has been done and what has not gotten done, what have we made and what have we missed. These thoughts permeate our minds at all times. The misses seem to weigh more heavily on us than what we have made happen in our lives. Be kind to yourself and remind yourself of the mini victories that are difference makers in your life.

I remember being accepted into the graduate program at Boston University. I was elated. I had just finished my undergraduate degree at Tennessee State University and knew there was more education I wanted to obtain. Boston was the furthest east and the coldest climate I'd ever lived in, and once I got there, I was uncertain. I was coming from a historical Black college. At Boston University, I was the only Black woman in three of my four classes.

I was lonely. It was difficult to make new friends. I felt as though I didn't fit. I must say, this led to my confidence decreasing, and I was contemplating if this was the place for me. At one point, I thought about leaving and not finishing.

I started to rationalize my thinking, making statements like: Grad school at this university was too expensive. I didn't really need another degree; many of my friends started working in media right after undergrad. I would have fewer school loans to pay back— and on and on and on.

And then there was my Aunt Carmen, in Boston, who I was living with while I was in school. She had earned her master's in broadcast journalism at BU too, and she repeatedly reminded me that if you can make it on the East Coast, you can make it anywhere. And then there was another valued voice, my mother, who always reminded me that only the strong survive, and I would be just fine. I didn't want to be known as a quitter. I wanted to finish what I started. I learned to overcome adversity, face my fears, and not easily flee from them.

I decided to finish what I started, and I did, graduating in the two short years allotted for the program. I left better than I came. Some of my greatest life lessons were during my graduate school years. It was there that I became a grown woman and learned to overcome many obstacles in life.

FINISHED WITH BABIES!!

Becoming a mother has clearly been the greatest accomplishment in my life. I have loved being a mom. I grew up with a family of 2 brothers and 1 sister. I had my first child at 32 and my last child at 38. A woman's body lets you know when having baby days are finished. The physiology of a woman varies from person to person; therefore, the knowledge is personal. The day my second child was born, I knew I wasn't finished and wanted more children. When my third was born, I knew we were done.

We had three children under 5 years old, and we were a loving, busy household. There is a 4-year difference between our first-born daughter and our second child and an eighteen-month difference between the second and third child. Yes, we had a 9- month-old and found out we were expecting another. Our emotions were everywhere — happy and sad at the same time. My sister and I are only thirteen months apart. I remember asking my mother how she dealt with having a 4-month old and getting the news that she was pregnant again. She responded, "I guess it was no big deal. I don't even remember!" That put me at ease.

When they were old enough, it was awesome being able to travel as a family with less baggage, no strollers, no bottles, and no diapers. The children could walk through the airport by themselves! I felt free. We were filled with exuberance. Yes, we were grateful for our family to be finished with the baby stages of life.

CHOICES

Sabrina: Finishers give themselves choices. When you lay down at night, you want to be able to say, *I'm proud of myself.* It's great to be praised by others, but when you can praise yourself, your confidence level is at a 10.

Reaching the highest position within Mary Kay Cosmetics, Inc., as a National Sales Director was a great finish, achieving the pinnacle of success. There are over 1 million people in our company: 150 active National Sales Directors in the US, and 18 are African American. Once the goal was finished and achieved, I quickly realized there is always more to do, more rankings to secure with the top of the top!

When you become a finisher in life, you create a life of options and opportunities. I think back to when I finished my undergraduate degree. If I didn't finish that undergrad degree, well, maybe I would not have gotten into the graduate program. And if I didn't finish my graduate program at Boston University, maybe I would not have gotten my first big journalism job at the Boston Globe newspaper. I believe finishing well gives you choices.

When I started my business in the cosmetics world, I knew that I didn't want to be just a salesperson. I wanted to move up the career path, travel to countries I had never been to, and build a global business, taking it to countries where women clearly needed and deserved to make above minimum wage. If I had not taken my US Mary Kay business to the highest heights, I would not have had the opportunity to grow it globally.

There is no way I could achieve this level of success alone. I had to master taking others with me across the finish line. I not only had to manage myself but also manage others. I was disciplined and determined to do what needed to be done; therefore, it was easier to show others the way. People see you more than they hear you, and I had to show the team what finishing looked like and felt like. Leadership is leading *your ship*. My team followed the leader, so it was important to give them a clear and valuable path to follow.

LEADERS FINISH WELL

Sabrina: Finishing as a strong leader always makes others follow, or it should. You do want to be a role model. You want to be the example that they not only hear but they see. People will hear you before they see you. I've always wanted to be the example for others to follow. In college, I wanted to go to class and encourage the party animals to do the same. In my business, I wanted to show up and show out. I didn't want to just do the basics. To make others believe, I had to show them what was possible.

There can be no leadership where there is no follow-ship. I keep that in the forefront of my mind. I never ask my sales organization to do anything that I have not been willing to do myself. I've built my business over the years with the premise that you must show the people where they can go, and they will grow!

Kenny: Finishing is one of the most important qualities to possess. My mother would always correct me and insist that I finish my sentences when I spoke. Just the basic thought of that makes you focus on finishing.

You can start with short-term, achievable goals and move toward big goals that sometimes appear impossible. They all have something very simple in common: a start day and a completion date. In the sport of wrestling, one of the essential elements is the art of finishing your moves to completion. That's when you score or maintain the advantage position. When you attend wrestling duals or tournaments, a common word you will hear yelled from the coaches, parents and teammates is "FINISH!"

Another important aspect is finishing your practice or training strong. The ability or the desire to finish your practice strong with intensity separates the good from the great, the winners from the losers. When you study the champions or the great business leaders, the one characteristic that stands out is their ability to finish what they start. Finishing is a habit!

For both of us, our parents taught us early on to finish what you start, whether it pertains to school, sports, or extracurricular activities. We were not allowed to quit.

That lesson was hard to understand in the beginning. I didn't see the benefits or the consequences from not finishing what I started. It was easy not to quit something that I enjoyed or was successful in. The hard part came when it wasn't fun, or I was on a team that wasn't winning. There were times when I didn't like the coach or I wasn't giving my best, and I didn't want to finish with that team. The rule was if you start, you were required to finish unless it was unhealthy, or the time didn't work out. As I grew older, it became clear why that concept was important, and the teaching helped shape us into who we are today, and now we have passed it onto the next generation.

We have also grown up with the old adage, "You are not finished when you are tired; you are finished when you are done."

Notes/Reflections

FORWARD

Kenny: I remember being fired from my job, my first time ever. Thinking back during that time, I wondered how I would move forward. I knew I would. I just wasn't sure how. The ability to move forward from difficulties in life takes courage and fortitude.

I've encountered some tough situations in my career. The job I was fired from was one of the best jobs I'd ever had. It was 2013, a year after coaching Coleman Scott to an amazing performance in the 2012 Olympic Games, earning him a bronze medal in London, England. After the Olympic Games, I was recruited to become head wrestling coach of an MMA team in Florida. They tripled my salary—an offer I couldn't refuse.

I was coaching some of the best fighters in the sport. Several of the athletes were in the UFC, and I was making a huge impact with the team. We won 10 fights in a row, only losing once. The owner of the team, the guy that hired me, started having financial issues along with infighting amongst some of the other coaches on the team.

Bottom line was the owner didn't want to honor the contract between us and felt I was getting paid too much. The team was winning, and the athletes and I thought things were going well. I had moved my family from Oklahoma to Florida for a job that I felt was secure, only a year prior. I knew when I decided to move forward in accepting this position, like with anything new, risk was involved. It was a calculated risk (with my family's blessings). I took it, always believing that if it didn't work out, I could always rebound and come back to the sport of wrestling. I just didn't think it would fall apart so soon. When I refused to take a pay cut, the owner fired me. No explanation or conversation. It was a very tough pill to swallow.

I remember leaving the office after getting the devastating news. How was I going to explain it to my wife and kids? How will we move forward? I got in my car and started driving home. I pulled over for a bit once I was out of sight of the office. I just had to get my head together because it was going in ten different directions.

I needed to get quiet and sit still for a bit and gather my thoughts.

Anytime in my life that I have been faced with adversity or even great triumphs, I lean on my faith to help me navigate through the challenges of life. In good times or bad, I always give thanks to God that I am still here and alive. This was surely one of those moments.

Once I cleared my head and accepted the fact that I was out of a job, I called my wife with the bad news. I arrived home and hugged my wife, and she immediately said everything would be alright, that we would overcome this setback. We then decided to call a family meeting with our three kids and tell them the news. Surprisingly, they handled it very well and just reiterated what their mom said: "Don't worry, dad! We got you, and everything will be alright."

Later that day, we decided to go get dinner and hit the beach, since we didn't know how much longer we were going to be in Florida. I remember walking along the beach and looking at the ocean and, to me, the future. I told the family that whatever God had in store for us, as long as we stayed together and kept believing in each other, no man or circumstance could stop us from being successful or keep us down. I am grateful for a supportive spouse and family that have always helped me get through tough times.

From that point on, the focus was to stay positive and know that sometimes God opens doors, and sometimes He closes them. To move forward and not be defeated, you just need to keep your head held high and believe there will be other opportunities that will come your way.

A couple of weeks later, I received a job offer in Texas and a new chapter in our lives began.

FIND YOURSELF TO FORWARD YOURSELF

You must take time to know who you are, what you want, where you want it, and on what terms. Don't move without looking within. To go forward, you must make up your mind and back it up with action. Have a plan of action that will catapult you into another place. Moving forward takes action, so make sure you are powering through the activities of your plan, one after the other. Put yourself on a path of progress: increase your credit score, increase your savings, build a bigger team, increase your sales, increase your net worth, increase your peace of mind, increase your joy— whatever path you choose, take action to move forward. Here are some ways we keep it moving forward:

1. Acknowledge you are not where you want or need to be.
2. Decide to do something about it.
3. Pray about it.
4. Let go.
5. Find your bigger reason and remind yourself of it daily.
6. Devise a plan with accountability.
7. Change your ways and create new habits.
8. Manage your mindset.
9. Get out of your comfort zone.
10. Stop overthinking it, and just do it!

I read this recently on Instagram: "If you do not like where you are, move. You are not a tree!" If you are not moving forward, you are standing still, so pull up your roots and get moving. Now, don't look back; that's not where you are going!

ACCEPT AND LET GO

Accepting what's happening in your life can be very painful. When certain life events happen, your raw emotions of anger, fear, and distrust, are real. You can be in a state of disbelief. Feelings of *why me?*

You might not always understand what life throws your way, so you must be flexible and understand that if God brings you to it, He will certainly bring you through it. Keep moving. Problems are opportunities to get stronger.

Acceptance of where you are and why is empowering. Instead of doubting and suffering when things don't go your way, dig deeper into a fuller understanding of why you are where you are at the current time. Don't dwell on the disappointment or deny that you are hurt or frustrated. Put your energy into pressing forward.

We spend lots of time planning our lives, chasing life, writing goals, and creating the plan. Don't let your 5year plan get in the way of a different path of progress. Plans are meant to be modified. Our plans are not always God's plan for our lives. It's important to not be excessively rigid with your plans, so allow God to be in control.

BE FREE TO BE!

As you continue moving forward, you will take complete ownership of your life because you possess the qualities of tough-mindedness and perseverance. Love yourself all the way to the top as you embrace both the lows and the highs. Your end result will reward every step of your climb.

If we approach life with an overly entitled attitude, thinking that life should be easier than it is, we are guaranteed to suffer. It's never easy to accept what life's challenges bring. These experiences cause us to feel vulnerable. It might be easier to shrink during these times and not want to fight for the life we deserve, but when we get up and keep moving forward, we will begin to see the rewards that lie ahead. Belief is the key to having a great life. If we believe there is a reason for life's challenges, then we will learn the lesson.

You often hear the phrase, "Fall forward to success." That means keep moving, there will be stumbles along the way.

Kenny: I remember the first time I received a bad grade on a spelling test. My first-grade teacher assured me that it wasn't the end of the world and with better studying and effort, I would be fine and would make it to the second grade. I was so disappointed in myself that it ruined the rest of my day. I was afraid of what my parents would say, but when I told them what happened, they weren't upset. They just said, "If you want better grades, you need to apply yourself and listen to your teachers." After my parents encouraged me to work harder, I focused on my spelling words, prepared myself for the next test, and got an A on the next one!

That was the first of many situations in life where I realized it's never as bad as you think. There is always light at the end of every dark tunnel. You must work at staying positive and not allow anything to keep you down for long. Having the ability to bounce back is key. The skill of moving forward is learning to think through the situation understanding that in most instances, there is a solution to the problem.

One of the earliest lessons in the skill of moving forward happened when I first started wrestling. Losing was something that I never cared much for; as a matter of fact, I despised it. I loved winning! As in any new sport endeavor, you're not going to be the best at it, so I took some losses. I noticed my competitors gained more confidence and got more satisfaction if they saw my negative emotions or if I dropped my head in defeat. Therefore, I changed my behavior and demeanor after a loss. I would keep my head held high, show no emotions, and take the attitude that I'd do better next time.

That mentality grew with me and paid dividends over the years. I became forward thinking, never looking back. I was always advancing, learning from my mistakes and becoming a student of performance. If something was broken, I'd pick up the pieces, put it back together, polish it up, and keep it moving forward.

One of the skills I became great at is never allowing the same techniques to be used on me twice. The ability to stay forward-thinking by overcoming setbacks and defeats allow you to continue to grow and build momentum as you strive to reach your goals. The most effective way to keep moving forward is your attitude. When you refuse to allow yourself to feel defeated even after a loss is when you understand how to be a winner.

When I look back on the things that kept me striving forward, I actually got more confidence with every loss. With every setback, I grew and learned more about myself. I began to develop a belief system that was rooted in my ability to utilize what I had learned from my past experiences and to use it as an advantage going forward. I would also study the champions or people that were advancing in their careers. I wanted to know their habits and watch their attitudes, how they treated or interacted with people. As a kid, I would watch the best wrestlers in the tournaments and noticed how they handled wins and close tough matches. I admire people who get up and keep going after the storm has passed, and I wanted to be that kind of person.

Remember, your setback is just a setup for a comeback. Wherever possible, focus your attention on what you want rather than what you don't have. Life can test you, but it can't break you. You're solid, you're resilient, and you're unstoppable. Be steady. Stay focused. Remember your purpose, and always press forward.

Notes/Reflections

Monday Family Travels

DISCLAIMER

Mary Kay Cosmetics, Inc.

Mary Kay Independent Beauty Consultants who reach the status of Mary Kay Independent Sales Directors can earn the use of a Cadillac XT5 (or cash in lieu of). The Cadillac program was started by Mary Kay Ash to reward the best of the best. Earning the use of a Pink Cadillac takes work and dedication. Approximately 1.5% of Mary Kay Independent Beauty Consultants reach the status of Independent Sales Director. Approximately 10% of Mary Kay Independent Sales Directors earn the use of the iconic Pink Cadillac.

Since the Mary Kay Career Car Program's inception in 1969, more than 171,000 independent sales force members have qualified or re-qualified to earn the use of a Mary Kay Career Car. There are currently over 3,600 Career Cars on the road nationwide, including over 1,000 Pink Cadillacs.

ACKNOWLEDGEMENTS

Thank you to Nathan True, our editor at Greenleaf Publishing Company for believing in our story and urging us along in the early days of writing this manuscript.

Thank you to Jackie "JC" Gardner from Blossom Literary Services for helping us put finishing touches on the book.

To our children, Sydnee, Kennedy, and Quincy for being our source of inspiration and to everyone who has crossed our path, for helping us become the people we are.

ABOUT THE AUTHORS

www.thegoldstandard.coach

Kenneth Dale Monday began wrestling at the age of six at a YMCA after-school program and excelled in the sport through high school and college, becoming a three-time All- American while at Oklahoma State University. After college, Kenny won Olympic Gold in Seoul, Korea in 1988, won Silver in Barcelona, Spain in 1992, and finished 6th in 1996 in Atlanta, Georgia. Kenny also won multiple Gold and Silver medals in World Cups, World Championships, and Pan-American events. After retiring from competition, Kenny became a highly respected wrestling coach. He is a member of the National Wrestling Hall of Fame, and the street where he attended the YMCA in his youth is now named after him: Kenny Monday Place. He's now the head wrestling coach at Morgan State University, the only HBCU D1 wrestling program in the country at this time.

Sabrina Goodwin Monday is a graduate of Tennessee State University and holds a master's degree from Boston University in broadcast journalism. She is a successful wife, mom, sister, friend, global mentor, and entrepreneur. She has hosted a daily radio show and has embraced a 30-plus year career in direct sales, climbing to the top of Mary Kay Cosmetics, Inc., as an Independent National Sales Director, driving many Pink Cadillacs over the years. She brings out the best in people, touching thousands of lives, and helping them tap into their God-given gifts by educating and encouraging them to grow mentally, spiritually, and financially.

They are the proud parents of three kind, loving, smart, fun young adults, who are college graduates. Sydnee, Howard University; Kennedy, University of North Carolina/ Chapel Hill; and Quincy, Princeton University. Building our family over the years has been our greatest challenge with our greatest rewards.

www.ingramcontent.com/pod-product-compliance
Lightning Source LLC
Chambersburg PA
CBHW060904120626
46553CB00001B/195